Tom Carty

The Jesus Reader

THE TEACHING AND IDENTITY OF JESUS CHRIST

the columba press

First edition, 2013, published by
the columba press
55A Spruce Avenue, Stillorgan Industrial Park,
Blackrock, Co. Dublin

Cover artwork and illustrations by Eve Anna Farrell
Origination by The Columba Press
Printed in Ireland by SPRINT-print

ISBN 978 1 85607 877 1

Many thanks to Phil Ibbs who introduced me to *Lectio Divina* and who leads the St Wulstan's meditation group with such insight. Thanks also to the members of the group who over the years have never failed to inspire, especially Mary Walker RIP.

Contents

Introduction

'Who do you say I am?'

For most people, whatever their beliefs, Jesus Christ is a fascinating and attractive figure. But who was he? This book sets out to answer the question through a selection of scriptural readings concentrating on his identity and teaching.

The most obviously accessible aspect of the gospels is Jesus' ethical teaching. Many who have no religious faith readily recognise him as a great and original moral teacher. He can be more demanding than the norms of his (and our) time, for example in his teaching on money (Readings 14.1 and 14.2) or divorce (see Luke 16:18), and his taking into account inner attitude, such as lust for the spouse of another, or anger (see Reading 10.1) rather than simply the external act (adultery or violence). On the other hand, he shows more flexibility and understanding than is usual in conventional morality, for example when he surprisingly does not condemn the adulterous woman who is dragged before him (Reading 12.2). These examples demonstrate the authority which we are told contemporaries noted. There is also an element of playful rhetorical exaggeration in his teaching meant to catch listeners unawares so they will think afresh about this subject (for example, Reading 14.1).

However, the same authors who bring us that sublime teaching also have definite views on his identity and these too are part of their overall message. To give a true account of Jesus' teaching, we have at the same time to do justice to who they thought he was. The book therefore has three specific aims:

1. Using their own words, give an idea of how Jesus' contemporary and near-contemporary followers expressed his identity.
2. Wherever possible, to allow his teaching to speak for itself.
3. To enable you to decide what Jesus Christ means to you, and to provide material for further thought.

Against that background, the book has been written with the overall aim of encouraging and enabling the reader to engage directly with scriptural texts. You can read the material in any order. It is presented thematically by chapter, each numbered consecutively, as are the individual readings. There are introductory notes on each chapter and detailed introductions to the two parts of the book, on Jesus' identity and his ethical teaching respectively.

You can read through or dip into it, but the suggestion is that you at least occasionally read one (or two if you prefer to combine shorter readings on the same topic) of the extracts in a concentrated way, and then spend just 15 to 20 minutes allowing what you have read to take your mind wherever it will. This simple technique of focused, reflective reading recognises that each reader brings something unique to a text. As aids to reflection, you will also find open-ended questions where appropriate, as well as some suggestions for the visualisation of scenes from the gospels. There is a short guide to focused reading in the next section, and, towards the end of the book, a summary of all the books of the Bible featuring in the readings or in the notes on each chapter. In the appendices you will also find notes on reading-based meditation, on using candles and icons as aids to focus in spiritual reading and a comprehensive glossary including a list of names.

The very word *reading* recognises the role of the reader in giving texts meaning. Each reader brings to the text his or her own unique experience and that is what makes focused reading so exciting. At the same time, especially in the case of books such as the Bible, you have to be aware that they have a history, and in reading extracts from it, you are entering a dialogue across the centuries. The introductions to Parts One and Two and the notes on each topic and on the individual readings provide you with some background and focus.

In the end, though, this book is about your personal reading of scripture. It is not primarily about Christian doctrine, and it was not written in an attempt to convert readers to any form of Christianity but in the conviction that it is culturally and spiritually important to know something about Jesus Christ, who he was and what he taught, and that the best way of doing that is to read the scriptures in an engaged and informed way. You can then come to your own conclusions about him.

Tom Carty, Easter, 2012

Focused Reading

Keeping an open mind

Try to come to the readings, even (or especially) to very familiar texts, as if for the first time: it is precisely when you think you know a text that you are probably missing something important. If you do not already know the scriptural readings in this book, it does not matter at all, in fact it could even be an advantage. Similarly, you do not need to be a believer to benefit from giving serious attention to the message about Jesus Christ or his ethical teaching. In either case, attentive reading followed by calm thought or meditation will ensure you get the most out of it. Bear in mind that this is about the interaction of the text with your life, experience and feelings, so even a one- or two-sentence extract could easily turn out to be packed with significance for you and provide ample raw material for your fifteen to twenty minutes.

How to go about reading

1. Take time to ensure you are physically and mentally relaxed before you begin. Empty your mind and do not pursue any thoughts that arise. This may prove difficult at first, but persevere, because with practice five minutes will normally be enough for you to get into the correct frame of mind, though you may need longer if you are particularly distracted or agitated. You may find an appropriate aid to relaxation and focus helpful, for example, a candle (see appendix two on candle meditation), if it is safe to light one.

2. Read slowly and deliberately (reading out loud prevents you from skimming the text). Pause a while before reading it through a second time, then cover it or put it aside until you need to check something or find a word or phrase.

3. Now let the reading or readings you have selected speak to you in silence for fifteen to twenty minutes. Give what you have read your full attention but let it approach you rather than the other way around, and be disciplined in focusing fully on what you have read, simply letting other, irrelevant, thoughts and sensations go without following them. The aim

is to go with the passage wherever it takes you. Sometimes you will need to be patient as nothing seems to be happening at first, while at other times a word, phrase or idea will instantly make a connection and you are on your way. And it does not necessarily have to be directly related to the subject of the reading: the text is your starting point, not your goal. If your meditation reaches a natural end, or is getting nowhere at all, you can use the suggested word or phrase in bold letters in the text of each reading instead. There is nothing sacred about 15-20 minutes, if you find that less or more time suits you better, trust your instinct. However, it is probably best to stick to a fixed period of time once you have found what suits you.

4. You will be asked to *visualise* a couple of scenes, as if witnessing for yourself what is described. It is also a good idea to spend a little time after your reading session taking stock of what has come out of it. To help you focus on issues raised in the reading, you will find occasional open-ended *questions* marked with a Q.

The Scriptural Sources

Based originally on oral traditions and written collections of sayings, and associated with different early Christian communities, the four gospels were probably written between the 60s (Mark) and the AD 90s (John). The first three, Mark, Matthew and Luke, known as the synoptic gospels, overlap in their accounts and sources and, despite variations in style and perspective, handle the material in similar ways. The fourth (John), although recognisably telling the same overall story, is quite different in style and probably represents a separate tradition. The earliest of Paul's letters (sometimes called epistles) to various churches and individuals were written in the AD 50s, well before the first gospel. Jesus is thought to have died in about AD 33.

Thanks to the work of generations of biblical scholars, we have a good idea of how the gospels came to be written. The first Christians preserved, meditated on, selected and shaped the oral traditions and written materials they received, typically in the form of collections of sayings and self-contained narrative episodes. They did so in the light of their beliefs about Jesus as members of one of the early church communities. Eventually, as the first two Christian generations began to disappear, it was felt that more structured written accounts were needed. These came to be known as gospels, a word meaning 'good news', which originally applied to the message itself, but which was transferred to the books containing the message (see notes to reading 9.1). The gospels are primarily testimonies to the faith of Jesus' early followers rather than full accounts of his life or even of his ministry:

> Now Jesus did many other signs in the presence of his disciples which are not written in this book. But these are written so that you may come to believe that Jesus is the Messiah, the Son of God, and that through believing you may have life in his name. (John 20:30–31)

So the author's purpose in writing a gospel was to convince the reader of Jesus' identity as 'Son of God'. However, this does not mean that the evangelists wrote pure propaganda. Luke introduces his book, consisting of the gospel bearing his name and the Acts of the Apostles, the chronicle of the early days of the church, by stressing his serious intent and concern for the reliability of his sources:

> Just as they (the accounts) were handed on to us by those who from the beginning were eyewitnesses and servants of the word, I too decided, after investigating everything carefully from the very first, to write an orderly account …(Lk 1:23)

What we have to realise is that the gospels are focused on the theological meaning of what Jesus says and what happens to him, and we learn about his personal life only on the relatively rare occasions when a biographical detail comes up incidentally as part of a saying or story included for its theological significance (such as his attitude to his family: see Chapter 9). Despite that, it is possible to make out a recognisable and impressive individual in these gospel extracts. In particular, Jesus emerges as a remarkable healer and an outstanding storyteller and teacher with a distinctive voice and a gift for vivid phrases and unexpected images, sometimes humorous. He impresses those who hear him speak with the authority both of his presence and of his message and attracts many followers and great crowds. He is also generous and open-minded, ignoring common prejudices and the 'unclean' status attached to certain professions and groups. He is courageous in disputing, in word and deed, interpretations of the law he considers inadequate or demonstrating false priorities.

In addition to these characteristics, there is something more about him. That something is what makes the question of his identity so important to the evangelists (the authors of the gospels) and so fascinating to us.

The world vividly reflected in the gospels can often make very different assumptions from ours about life and death, sickness, human behaviour and society. We have to be sensitive to those differences if we are to relate to what they tell us. What is more, the Bible is not a single book, it is more like a library and you can easily lose your way and become discouraged without a guide and a specific goal in reading it. The goal here is to learn something about what Jesus taught and who he was thought to be, while the guide is a set of carefully selected and mostly short biblical readings.

PART ONE

THE IDENTITY OF JESUS CHRIST

Part One: Outline

Part One: Introduction

Preludes
>Introductory Readings
>1. Mark 1:9–11
>2. Luke 1:30–35

MAIN READINGS

Chapter One: Seeking the Face of God
>1.1 Psalm 27
>1.2 Isaiah 55:8–9
>1.3 Psalm 139:1–4, 13, 16, 17

Chapter Two: Incarnation

(a) The Word of God	2.1 Genesis 1:1–3
	2.2 Psalm 19:1–4, 7–8, 14
	2.3 Jeremiah 1:4–5, 7, 9
	2.4 Deuteronomy 30:11–14
	2.5 Isaiah 29:13
	2.6 Hebrews 4:12–13
(b) The Only Son	2.7 John 1:1, 14
	2.8 Hebrews 1:1–3
	2.9 John 1:14, 17–18
	2.10 Matthew 17:1–8
	2.11 Galatians 3:26–29
(c) Light of the World	2.12 John 1:3–5, 9
	2.13 Isaiah 59:9–11
	2.14 Isaiah 60:1
	2.15 John 12:44–47
(d) Overview	2.16 John 1:1–18

Chapter Three: Messiah
>3.1 Luke 4:16–21
>3.2 Matthew 21:9–13
>3.3 Matthew 21:33–40

Part One: Introduction

Who was Jesus Christ? How did his followers see him? He was certainly remembered as having been a remarkable *teacher*: 'All the people were spellbound by what they heard' (Lk 19:48), and the second part of this book is devoted to his ethical teaching in particular. As for his identity, he cautiously or even hesitantly, accepted the designation *Messiah*, the title of the long-awaited deliverer of the Jewish people. We take a detailed look at this aspect of his identity, remembering that Jesus lived and died a faithful Jew.

It is often forgotten that he was also a *healer* of physical, mental and spiritual ailments, so that will be the next area we look at. We then turn to the accounts of the events of the first Easter, at Jesus as *Suffering Servant* and *Risen Lord*, and finally to his *sacramental presence* in the Eucharist or Holy Communion, which he requested his followers to celebrate in his memory. However, the core of this exploration of his identity is devoted to the *incarnation*: the idea outlined in the prologue of St John's gospel (Reading 2.16) that in Jesus the Word of God took on fleshly, that is truly human, form. What this signifies for John is only part of the story: committed to writing to persuade us of Jesus' unique identity (see Jn 20:31), it remains a living, challenging text to which we can respond.

Jesus' identity in the New Testament

In fact, there is no shortage of attempts in the scriptures at describing or defining Jesus' identity. While the church's developed teaching on the nature of Christ was not settled, because of bitter disputes, until as late as the fourth and fifth centuries (Councils of Nicea AD 325, and Chalcedon AD 451), it is in essence present in the various letters and gospels which reflect the faith of the first century Christians who wrote and preached about it. Later generations had to refine and define doctrine more explicitly in the light of subsequent controversy, and reconcile the implications of different statements in the scriptures. However, in outline the picture is clear enough: For the authors of the New Testament Jesus expresses, makes visible or makes known what God is. He addresses God as his Father and in St John's gospel, typically more explicit than the three synoptic gospels, goes so far as to say 'Whoever has seen me has seen the Father' (Jn 14:8) and 'The Father and I are one' (Jn 10:30), although he also says in the same gospel that 'The Father is greater than I' (Jn 14:28), which does not necessarily contradict the other two statements.

He is addressed as Rabbi or Teacher and Lord, and he refers to himself as the Son of Man, but not directly as Son of God. He is also the Lamb of God, the King of Israel, the Holy One of God, the Messiah, the Word (of God), the only Son, and the Son of God; all according to St John's gospel. In the synoptic gospels, he is called variously a prophet, Emmanuel (meaning 'God-is-with-us'), the Son of David, and the Christ or Messiah, the Son of the Most High and the Son of God.

In the letters of the New Testament he is described, among other things, as 'The one mediator between God and humankind' (1 Tim 2:5), but also as 'The image of the invisible God' (Col 1:15), and 'The radiant light of God's glory and the perfect copy of his nature' (Heb 1:3). St Paul summarises by saying that 'In him the fullness of God was pleased to dwell' (Col 1:10). In these highly expressive images, Paul is drawing on Old Testament Wisdom literature (see section 2.1). Indeed, he refers to Christ as 'The power and *wisdom* of God' (1 Cor 1:24).

In addition to these many statements about Jesus' identity, the series of what are referred to as 'I am' statements distil the fourth gospel's presentation of who he is. Using striking first-person statements, it defines him as the bread of life (Jn 6:35, see also Readings 6.2 and 7.1); the light of the world (Jn 8:12, see Readings 2.9–2.12); and the resurrection and the life (Jn 11:24, as in Readings 6.1 and 6.2).

Another of the 'I am' statements (Jn 14:6) sums up Jesus' identity as 'The way, the truth and the life' (that is, the way to God, the truth about God, life in God), and his gospel also has Jesus uttering the ultimate 'I am' statement when, in reply to some in his audience asserting that Abraham is their father, and not the one Jesus calls Father, he says, 'Very truly I tell you, before Abraham was, I am' (Jn 8:58). Using *I am* in this way as an absolute statement is how the holy name of God is expressed in the Jewish scriptures. His furious audience pick up rocks and are about to stone him for what they consider to be blasphemy, while Jesus has to hide until it is safe to leave the Temple.

Only once in the gospels is he directly referred to or addressed as God, at the end of St John's gospel when Thomas, doubting Thomas, recognises the risen Jesus (Jn 20:28; see Chapter 6 notes). Elsewhere in the fourth gospel, Jesus maintains a distinction between himself and God, and not just the Father: 'And this is eternal life, that they may know you, the only true God, and Jesus Christ whom you have sent' (Jn 17:3).

At various times since the nineteenth century scholars and theologians have tried to get behind what they call the 'Christ of faith' to find the supposedly hidden 'real' Jesus of history but it has proved impossible to separate out the two aspects in such a straightforward way. The gospels are written from a position of faith and everything in them is there because it is considered to have some relevance to that perspective. We learn nothing about Jesus' life between babyhood and the age of twelve, when he is found by his parents debating with learned rabbis in the Temple. Then there is silence once more until he is about thirty and ready to launch his mission. Filling out the details of Jesus' biography is simply not a priority for the evangelists. That does not mean we cannot draw conclusions of our own from his words or behaviour (see Reading 5.2 on the episode in the Garden of Gethsemane, for example), just that the authors of the gospels do not consider questions of general biography, personality or psychology as particularly relevant to their task.

When does Jesus become aware of his identity?
That raises the question as to whether there is a moment when Jesus becomes fully aware of his identity or whether he always believes he has a unique relationship with the Father. One obvious candidate for such a moment of insight would be his baptism by John as he begins his ministry (see Introductory Reading 1 from Mark, also Matthew 3:13–17; Luke 3:15–18, 21–22; John

1:24–34 if you wish to compare the different versions of this event as an interesting example of all four gospels handling the same or similar material). The account culminates in the descent of the Holy Spirit and the proclamation from above that Jesus is God's beloved Son. Those two features are subjective in Mark, but are seen and heard by others in Matthew: 'This is my son' (Mt 3:17). In the fourth gospel John the Baptist rather than the narrator vouches for what happened. The spiritual meaning of the episode is clear and it acquires extra power and dignity presented as a public event rather than a personal experience. The similar divine endorsement of Jesus as the beloved son at the transfiguration (Reading 2.10) is a confirmation of his status and identity to the disciples and by extension to the readers: 'Listen to him!' (Mk 9:7; Mt 17.5; Luke 9:35).

What about the Annunciation to Mary by the angel in Luke? He tells her she will be the mother of the Messiah, who will be called the Son of God (see Introductory Reading 2), could that not be the moment? Luke's infancy narrative, of which this is a part, is wonderfully told but the story appears only in this gospel (in Matthew, the angel appears to Joseph, Mary's betrothed: Mt 1:18–25), and in a section which was evidently regarded as semi-detached from the rest. It is not referred to directly again, despite its considerable spiritual power (significantly it has been a favourite subject of artists throughout the centuries). Just as you could argue logically for the annunciation, that is, Jesus' conception, as the moment the incarnation becomes reality, you could make out a similar case for his birth, with the symbolism of the chorus of angels proclaiming his identity to the poor of the land (Lk 2:8–14), and the three learned gentiles coming to pay him homage (Mt 2:11–12). Then Simeon and the prophet Anna rejoice in the birth of the Messiah when Mary and Joseph bring the child to the Temple (Lk 2:25–35; 36–38; see also Preludes chapter). All of these details are to be found in the two self-contained infancy narratives, in which the author is concerned above all to demonstrate that Jesus is the Messiah foretold by the prophets. Yet none of them carry over into the main body of the gospel.

For Paul, on the other hand, it is through the resurrection that Jesus' inherent status as Son of God becomes operative. He, Paul, is preaching, he says, the gospel of God, 'Concerning his Son, who was descended from David according to the flesh and was declared to be *Son of God in power* ... by resurrection from the dead.' (Rom 1:3–4). John however has no need for sudden realisation or revelation as his Jesus is confident in his identity throughout. He is the Word of God made flesh: 'In the beginning was the Word, and the Word was with God, and the Word was God' (Jn 1:1: see Reading 2.16). We shall be looking at both the resurrection (Chapter 6) and the concept of the Word (Chapter 2a) later.

Familiar and new metaphors

It would be for the church to take these various approaches and make out of them a coherent doctrine on the identity of Jesus Christ. That proved a difficult and contentious task, but out of that process came eventually the teaching that Jesus Christ was both 'True God and true man'. Our aim here however is to look at what was and is written in the scriptures which provided the raw material for the teaching of the church. Naturally enough the authors turned to familiar imagery when dealing with the phenomenon of Jesus Christ: the Word of God, metaphors of light and darkness, the personification of Wisdom, the figure of the Servant of the Lord/Suffering Servant among them. All of these played a significant part in Jewish spirituality and we trace them back to the Old Testament (see Chapter 2).

On the other hand, a radically new term or image probably was necessary to convey how his identity was perceived. The designation 'Only Son of the Father' or, to put it less awkwardly, 'Son of God', was potentially a radical departure for Judaism, given its fierce suspicion of anything that seemed to dilute monotheism. The question remains as to what those who use this term understand by it. Does each author understand it in the same way, and do they all use it consistently? Unlikely, but precisely what the authors mean is in the end unknowable. In the chapters and readings which follow, we shall explore their various attempts to express what they saw as a unique relationship.

Gospel references
Mt 1:18–25; 2:11–12; 3:13–17
Mk 1:1–9
Lk 2:8–14; 2:25–38; 3:15–18, 21–22
Jn 1:1, 24–34; 6:35, 8:12, 58; 10:30, 11:25; 14:6–9, 28; 17:3; 20:28–31

Preludes

Nathanael replied, 'Rabbi, you are the Son of God, the King of Israel.'
Jn 1:49

All four gospels begin their accounts of Jesus' ministry with his baptism in the River Jordan by John the Baptist after which a voice from above proclaims him as the beloved Son.

Introductory Reading 1:
He saw the Spirit descending

In those days Jesus came from Nazareth of Galilee and was baptised by John in the Jordan. And just as he was coming up out of the water, he saw the heavens torn apart and the Spirit descending like a dove on him. And a voice came from heaven, 'You are my son, the *Beloved*; with you I am well pleased' (Mk 1:9–11). *(Note that here in Mark's version of this experience only Jesus sees the descent of the spirit and hears the endorsement from the heavens.)*

Mark's gospel certainly has the most effective opening of the four, plunging straight into the action with this dramatic scene, which is introduced in the preceding verses by the fierce figure of John the Baptist dressed in camel's hair and nourishing himself in the desert on locusts. As Jesus will later, he is calling everybody urgently to repentance but unlike Jesus, he uses baptism to symbolise it. Despite his being in the Judean desert, great crowds come streaming out of Jerusalem to confess their sins and be cleansed in the waters of the River Jordan. This is the lively scene that Jesus enters in preparation for the start of his ministry, heralded by the Baptist. The words from the cloud have echoes of a combination of Psalm 2:7: 'You are my son, today I have begotten you' and Isaiah's words about the Servant of the Lord (see Reading 5.1): 'Here is my servant, whom I uphold, my chosen, in whose name my soul delights; I will put my spirit upon him' (Isa 42:1).

The other three gospels all precede their account of, or in John's case reference to, the baptism with a prologue or introduction. In John this is an abstract yet poetic treatment of Jesus' identity as Word, Light and only Son (Reading 2.16), while Matthew and Luke detail the circumstances surrounding his conception and birth to demonstrate that he is the Messiah and is entitled to be called Son of David and Son of God (Mt 1 and 2; Lk 1 and 2). These stories are familiar to most of us from school nativity plays and the traditional Christmas crib, a visual summary centred on the infant Jesus of what the incarnation means. As with all of the infancy narrative in Luke, the story of the annunciation is full of references to the Old Testament and places Jesus in the lineage of King David, which amounts to saying he is the messiah. The significance of Mary being a virgin is that Jesus is then literally the son of God.

Introductory Reading 2:
The Annunciation
The angel said to her, 'Do not be afraid, Mary, for you have found favour with God. And now you will conceive ... and bear a son, and you will name him Jesus. He will be great and will be called the Son of the Most High, and the Lord God will give to him the throne of his ancestor David. He will reign over the house of Jacob for ever, and of his kingdom there will be no end.' Mary said to the angel, 'How can this be, since I am a virgin?' The angel said to her, 'The Holy Spirit will come upon you, and the power of the Most High will overshadow you, therefore the child to be born will be holy; he will be called Son of God.' *Lk 1:30–35*

Luke's prologue draws on images of light, applied to the coming of Jesus (see also Readings 2.12–2.15):

The dawn from on high will break upon us
to give light to those who sit in darkness
and in the shadow of death.

Zechariah, the priest, father of John the Baptist. (Lk 1:78–79)

My eyes have seen your salvation
which you have prepared in the presence of all peoples
a light for revelation to the Gentiles
and for glory to your people Israel.

Simeon thanking God he has lived to see the birth of the messiah (Lk 2:29–32).

In his Father's House

Apart from the account of a visit to Jerusalem when he was twelve years old, the gospels are silent about Jesus' life up to his baptism, presumably because that is the only story from those years which is of significance to the evangelist, given his priorities. The account of the visit has Jesus go missing to the great distress of his parents. They eventually find him in the Temple, discussing and debating (Lk 2:41–52). His reply to his relieved mother and father puzzles them: 'Why were you searching for me? Did you not know I must be in my father's house?' (Lk 2:49). This episode looks ahead to Jesus' final public appearances, also at Passover time, when he is in the Temple daily, teaching and healing in defiance of the priests and in ever-present danger of arrest (see Reading 3.3). It also testifies to a definite sense of a special relationship to God as he was emerging from childhood.

We learn nothing at all about his life for eighteen more years until John the Baptist is dramatically proclaiming his arrival and he accepts baptism at John's hands before being confirmed in his identity by his vision of the Holy Spirit's descent and the voice of God. Then, strengthened by a period of meditation alone in the desert during which he successfully counters temptation (*Mt 4:1–11*), he is ready to begin his mission. He chooses to do so in his home town of Nazareth (see Reading 3.1).

Gospel references
Mt   1:18–2:21; 4:1–11
Mk   1:1–11
Lk   1:26–56, 67–80; 2:1–39, 41–52

Chapter One

Seeking the Face of God

For it is the God who said 'Let light shine out of darkness' who has shone in our hearts to give the light of the knowledge of the glory of God in the face of Jesus Christ. 2 Cor 4:6

Assuming God exists, is he knowable? After all, an indifferent, unapproachable God is certainly imaginable. Does it make sense to try to approach him, never mind attempting to get to know him? Is it possible even to talk about him meaningfully and if so, what can be said?

Jesus was a faithful Jew and the background to his spiritual teaching was the Jewish Bible, to which he constantly referred. The Psalms cover every spiritual emotion, including the sense of God's absence. When the psalmist (Reading 1.1) wishes to express the desire for a closer relationship with him, he says he wants to see his face, indeed that he has been hiding his face. We know that this is a metaphor, God does not have a face, but we have to turn to metaphors if we are to speak at all about him. This metaphor is nonetheless meaningful: we recognise people principally by their face, it also expresses their inner emotions.

Even with the help of metaphors, the natural desire to know God, to approach him in some way, comes up against his sheer otherness and his forbidding holiness: 'Be still and know that I am God!' (Ps 46:18). Paradoxically, however, the daunting statement of the immense distance between humankind and God in Reading 1.2 comes in fact from a man speaking in his name, the prophet Isaiah, and just a couple of verses earlier he is encouraging individuals to seek a relationship with the same transcendent God: 'Seek the Lord while he may be found; call upon him while he is near ...' (Isa 55:6).

All that is required is the courage or faith to be active in seeking him: 'The Lord is near to all who call on him.' (Ps 145:18), because those who seek him will find him: 'I sought the Lord, and he answered me and delivered me from all my fears' (Ps 33:4), and even if we do find it difficult to approach him, the psalmist reassures us that he already knows each of us individually. Here, in a song of confidence in God, rather than being discouraged or frightened by his power and presence, he finds them a source of wonder and delight (Reading 1.3).

In the Old Testament humankind is nonetheless caught between the two poles of God's *transcendence* (his immeasurable distance from us, his total otherness) and his *immanence* (presence and nearness). In the New Testament, as we shall see, Jesus is seen as bridging that gap: his identity is defined in terms of his unique relationship to God, or the Father as he called him. As the living Word of God, Jesus expresses and communicates what is meant by 'God', he alone makes God knowable. So the psalmist's prayer that he may see the face of God is answered in the person of Jesus Christ. In fact St Paul uses a similar metaphor about Jesus' identity when he speaks of 'God's glory in the face of Jesus Christ' (2 Cor 4:6).

Reading 1.1
Hide not your face

> Hear, O Lord, when I cry aloud,
> be gracious to me and answer me.
> 'Come,' my heart says, *'seek his face.'*
> Your face, O Lord, I do seek.
> Do not hide your face from me.
> *Ps 27*

Reading 1.2
My thoughts are not your thoughts

> For my thoughts are not your thoughts,
> nor are your ways my ways, says the Lord.
> For as the heavens are higher than the earth,
> so are my ways *higher* than your ways
> and my thoughts than your thoughts.
> *Isa 55:8–9*

Reading 1.3
You know me

> O Lord, you have *searched me* and known me,
> You know when I sit down and when I rise up,
> you discern my thoughts from far away …
> Even before a word is on my tongue, O Lord,
> you know it completely …
> For it was you that formed my inward parts,
> you knit me together in my mother's womb …
> In your book were written
> all the days that were formed for me
> when none as yet existed.
> How weighty to me are your thoughts O God!
> How vast is the sum of them!
> Ps 139:1–4, 13, 16, 17

Chapter Two

Incarnation

The Word became flesh and lived among us. Jn 1:14
One way of exploring how Jesus Christ is portrayed by the authors of the New Testament is to examine the language they use about him. We begin by considering three images from the prologue to St John's gospel: the Word, the Only Son and the Light of the World.

(a) The Word (of God)

The term incarnation comes from a Latin word meaning 'taking human form'. The idea behind it can be found in the prologue to St John's gospel in which Jesus is described as the Word become flesh. The term 'Word of God' occurs frequently in the Old Testament, typically meaning the Law or the prophets. However, the idea of Jesus being the Word of God draws principally on a different Jewish tradition, that of Wisdom.

Old Testament images and ideas
Like Paul when describing Jesus' identity (extract A; see also Introduction to Part I), John was able to draw on the rich resources of Old Testament Wisdom literature from the books of Proverbs, Wisdom, and Ecclesiasticus/Sirach for his idea of the Word (extracts B and C). The metaphors which Paul and the author of Hebrews employ in their letters to give an idea of Jesus' identity are directly influenced by the language used in Wisdom: for example, compare: 'The power and wisdom of God' (1 Cor 1:24), 'The radiant light of God's glory', and 'The perfect copy of his nature' (both Heb 1:3), and 'The image of the invisible God' (Col 1:15) with this extract from the book of Wisdom:

A She is a breath of *the power of God,*
    And a pure emanation of *the glory of the Almighty,*
    She is a reflection of eternal *light,*
    A *spotless mirror* of the working of God,
    and an *image* of his goodness. *Wis 7:25–26*

In John's case, it is less the language which reflects the Wisdom books of the Old Testament than the idea of the personified Word itself, coming from the mouth of God as in the next example (in both the following, it is Wisdom herself who speaks):

B I came forth from the mouth of the Most High,
    and covered the earth like a mist,
    I dwelt in the highest heavens …
    Sir 24:3–4

And here, on being, like the Word, with God 'In the beginning', actually assisting in the creation. As John puts it about the Word: 'All things came into being through him' (Jn 1:2):

C When he established the heavens, I was there,
    when he drew a circle on the face of the deep,
    when he assigned to the sea its limit …
    When he marked out the foundations of the earth,
    then I was beside him …
    Prov 8:27–30

Examining the metaphor

Let's look in more detail at this metaphor. Think of some common expressions in which the term 'word' occurs, for example:

- is there any word of where he is?
- to give/keep one's word
- to put something into words
- to have a word with somebody
- to put in a good word for somebody
- to be word-perfect

Q. Do you think any of them could apply in this context?

The Bible begins with a metaphor of God's creative word, and the first thing created is light, itself used extensively in the Old

Testament in connection with God or his word: 'Then God said, "Let there be light"; and there was light' (Reading 2.1). In turn, that creation itself is seen in the psalms as an expression of God: the words *'telling'*, *'proclaims'*, *'speech'*, *'declares'*, and *'voice'* all continue the metaphor (Reading 2.2). It is also significant that the second half of this psalm is about the *Law*, the first five books of the Bible, including the commandments. This is more concretely the 'word of God', as are the words of the *prophets* who speak in his name: Reading 2.3, Jeremiah's account of his calling, demonstrates how literally the prophets took their role as vehicles for the word of the Lord.

The Law and the prophets are not to remain dead letters. As Jesus does when describing the new covenant proposed by God (see the notes to Reading 7.1), Moses stresses that the ten commandments must be transferred into the hearts of men and women (Reading 2.4). If this does not happen, their professions of faith will be no more than empty phrases.

Reading 2.1
In the beginning
In the beginning God created the heavens and the earth; the earth was a formless void and darkness covered the face of the deep, while the spirit of God swept over the face of the waters. Then *God said* 'Let there be light'; and there was light. *Gen 1:1–3*

Reading 2.2
The heavens speak of God

> The heavens are telling the glory of God
> and the firmament proclaims his handiwork.
> Day to day pours forth speech,
> and night to night declares knowledge.
> There is no speech, nor are there words …
> Yet their voice goes out through all the earth.
>
> … The law of the Lord is perfect, *reviving the soul*;
> the decrees of the Lord are sure, making wise the simple;
> the precepts of the Lord are right, rejoicing the heart …
> Let the words of my mouth and the meditation of my heart
> be acceptable to you, O Lord, my rock and my redeemer.
> *Ps 19:1–4, 7–8, 14*

Reading 2.3
The calling of a prophet

> Before *I formed you* in the womb I knew you;
> And before you were born I consecrated you;
> I appointed you a prophet to the nations.
> Now the word of the Lord came to me saying,
> 'You shall go to all to whom I send you,
> and you shall speak whatever I command you'
> … then the Lord put out his hand and touched my mouth;
> and the Lord said to me,
> 'Now I have put my words in your mouth …' *Jer 1:4–5, 7, 9*

Readings 2.4 to 2.6 all insist that the word of God must penetrate to the heart if it is to have any effect.

Reading 2.4
The word of God is in your heart
Surely, this commandment … is not too hard for you, nor is it too far away. It is not in heaven, that you should say, "Who will go up to heaven for us, and get it for us so that we may hear it and observe it?" Neither is it beyond the sea, that you should say, "Who will cross to the other side of the sea for us and get it for us so that we may hear it and observe it?" No, *the word is very near you*; it is in your mouth and in your heart. *Deut 30:11–14*

Reading 2.5
Their hearts are far from me
The Lord then said '… This people approaches me only in words, honours me only with *lip-service* while their hearts are far from me, and reverence for me, as far as they are concerned, is nothing but human commandment, a lesson memorised.' *Isa 29:13*

The Word in the New Testament
If we give only *lip-service* to God, as the prophet Isaiah puts it and are insincere in our expressions of devotion, we will be found out because the Word of God will put us to the test and we will be exposed (Reading 2.6). Jesus said he had not come to abolish the Law and the Prophets but to fulfil or complete them (Mt 5:17) and in the New Testament the Word of God is to be found not

primarily in the text of the Law or the words of an intermediary like Isaiah or Jeremiah but directly in the form of a person who enjoys a unique relationship with God. According to the gospel of Saint John, Jesus Christ is the Word: he perfectly expresses what God is. You could put it more vividly by saying that when God speaks to us what he says is 'Jesus' (Reading 2.7). This is what became known as the incarnation.

Reading 2.6
Sharper than a sword
The word of God is living and active, sharper than any two-edged sword, piercing until it divides soul from spirit, joints from marrow; it is able to judge the thoughts and intentions of the heart. And before him no creature is hidden, but all are naked and *laid bare. Heb 4:12–13*

Reading 2.7
The Word became flesh
In the beginning was the Word and the Word was with God and the Word was God. He was in the beginning with God ... and the Word became flesh *and lived among us*, and we have seen his glory ... *Jn 1:1, 14*

(b) The only Son (of God)

There is a second powerful image in the Prologue to St John's gospel, the very concrete one of an only Son. The message of the New Testament is that in his very person Jesus Christ makes the living God known. If we want to know what God is like, we must turn to Jesus, the image of his Father and so the perfect reflection of the invisible God's glory.

The term 'Son of God' is used very sparingly in the gospels. If you take the oldest, that of Mark, apart from in the opening verse (where some versions omit it anyway), there are just five occasions on which it is used, each an important moment in his account of Jesus' ministry. It is never used by Jesus himself in the synoptic gospels and only once in the fourth gospel, and then indirectly (see below). On two occasions it features in divine proclamations of Jesus' identity, one at his baptism (see Reading 1 in the Preludes section) and the other at the transfiguration (Reading 2.10), in other words one at the start of his ministry and the other near the end, before Jesus goes to Jerusalem to meet his fate. The other three occasions also come at each end of the story: one at the beginning, when 'unclean spirits' recognise his power as Son of God (Mk 3:11), and the other two near, and at, the very end respectively: the first during his interrogation by the high priest, who asks him if he is the Son of the Blessed One (Mk 14:61–62), the second, on the lips of the gentile centurion in charge at the crucifixion who recognises Jesus for who he is at the moment of his death (Mk 15:39). Matthew has a few additional occasions on which Jesus is referred to or addressed as the Son of God but typically these are in places in the text where Mark and Luke have 'Messiah' or 'the Christ', so it seems likely that Matthew deliberately substituted the one term for the other when editing his source.

In John's gospel 'The Son' is frequently used by Jesus when referring to himself, as are 'The Father' and 'My Father' in referring to God, indeed the two terms Father and Son constitute a distinctive theme of this gospel. 'Son of God' is rarer, occurring six times. For example, in the mouth of John the Baptist recounting what happened at Jesus' baptism, which parallels the other gospels (Jn 1:30–34); or later when Jesus defends himself against accusations of blasphemy and in doing so gives an idea of how the term is used in this gospel at least. He had said that 'The Father and I are one' (Jn 10:30) and when the crowd react as if to stone him for blasphemy he asks:

> Can you say that the one whom the Father has sanctified and sent into the world is blaspheming because I said '*I am God's Son*'? If I am not doing the works of my Father, then do not believe me. But if I do them, even though you do not believe me, believe the works, so that you may know and understand that the Father is in me, and I am in the Father (Jn 10:36–38).

His use of the term here remains (perhaps deliberately) unclear and ambiguous, because the strange thing is that he had not called himself Son of God at all, what he had said was that he and the Father were one, so presumably he regarded the two expressions as amounting to the same thing. The final example of the use of this term seems to equate the title with being the Messiah, when the author of the gospel states his purpose in writing it as being to convince the reader that Jesus was the 'Messiah, the son of God' (Jn 20:30).

Son of the Father

What exactly did the evangelists mean when they used the term? Jesus called God *Abba*, beloved Father, so in terms of that relationship, he is indeed the son of God. The implications of the imagery of father and son are primarily of identity, intimacy and love, a concrete, unique, personal relationship. The human father/son relationship has two aspects, the one biological (as we would put it now, a son shares his father's DNA), the other social and emotional. We commonly refer to similarities of appearance ('he is the image of his father'), as well as of behaviour and temperament or personality ('like father, like son') and both of these aspects are present in the metaphor. Jesus' relationship with the Father logically means he is uniquely placed to make him known.

Readings 2.8 and 2.9 are rich in meaning and repay close attention. They can be considered together or separately. According to Reading 2.8, the role of the prophets had been, to use light imagery, to serve as 'A lamp shining in a dark place', but they recede into the background once the light of Christ has dawned and 'the morning star rises in your hearts' (2 Pet 1:19). In Reading 2.9 St John says Jesus completes the work of Moses, a significant claim given Moses' status as the bringer of the Law and the patriarch of his people. In fact one of the most dramatic episodes in the gospels expresses the relationship visually: the *transfiguration* (Reading 10), when his three closest followers see Jesus bathed in heavenly light (light again!) in a foretaste of the resurrection. In this vision he is seen conversing with Moses and Elijah, who represent the Law and the prophets respectively, now seen to be pointing to, or preparing the ground for, Jesus, who completes or fulfils their work. It all culminates in his endorsement as Son of the Father just before he goes up to Jerusalem for the last days of his ministry and the terrible ordeal he knows he must face there. This episode parallels the similar endorsement after his baptism at the very start of his mission (see Introductory Reading 1 in the Preludes section).

Postscript

The good news according to Paul is that the sonship of Christ has important implications for all of us: we can become adopted sons and daughters of God through faith in Jesus (Reading 2.11), a message also found in the prologue to St John's gospel (Jn 1:12–13, Reading 16).

Q *According to the next two Readings, the Son is greater than the prophets or the Lawgiver Moses. If Jesus makes God known, what does that tell us about what God is like?*

Reading 2.8
The Son completes the prophets
Long ago God spoke to our ancestors in many and various ways by the prophets, but in these last days he is has spoken to us by a son ... He is the *reflection* of God's glory and the exact imprint of God's very being. *Heb 1:1–3*

Reading 2.9
Jesus and Moses
We have seen his glory, the glory as of a father's only son, full of grace and truth. The law, indeed, was given through Moses; grace and truth came through Jesus Christ. No one has ever seen God. The only Son, who is close to the Father's heart, *has made him known. Jn 1:14, 17–18*

Reading 2.10
'Listen to him!'
Jesus took with him Peter and James and his brother John and led them up a high mountain, by themselves. And he was transfigured before them, and his face shone like the sun, and his clothes became dazzling white. Suddenly there appeared to them Moses and Elijah, talking with him ... A bright cloud overshadowed them all and from the cloud a voice said, 'This is my Son, the Beloved, with him I am well pleased, listen to him!' When the disciples heard this, they fell to the ground and were overcome by fear. Then Jesus came and touched them, saying, 'Get up and do not be afraid.' And when they looked up, they saw no-one except *Jesus* himself, *alone. Mt 17:1–8*

Reading 2.11
All children of God
In Christ Jesus you are all children of God through faith. As many of you as were baptised into Christ have clothed yourselves with Christ. There is no longer Jew or Greek, there is no longer slave or free, there is no longer male and female; for *all of you are one* in Christ Jesus. *Gal 3:26–29*

(c) The Light of the world

'The darkness is passing away and the true light is already shining' (1 Jn 2:8).

The prologue to St John's gospel contains a third metaphor, expressing the identity of Jesus Christ as *light*. (Reading 2.12) As we saw in the last section, the Bible begins with the creation of light and Jesus is bathed in heavenly light at the transfiguration. The image occurs throughout the Old and New Testaments: 'Your word is a lamp to my feet and a light to my path' (Ps 119:105); 'I have come as light into the world, so that everyone who believes in me should not remain in the darkness' (Jn 12:46, see Reading 2.16).

First, think for a couple of minutes of some of the associations of light and darkness, for example:

- She was the light of my life
- To shed light on something
- To enlighten, illuminate
- To light the way for somebody
- The powers of darkness
- They've kept me in the dark about it

Q Do any of these examples of the metaphor in use fit this context? See what you think after the next set of Readings.

The Jewish people bemoaned the fate of their proud but small and vulnerable country, as disaster was piled upon disaster and one occupying power followed another. They yearned for a messiah, a Son of David who would dispel the darkness and restore Israel. The coming of the light was a frequently used metaphor expressing this messianic hope and, since Christians recognised Jesus

Christ as the Messiah, the prophecies were applied to him and are particularly associated with Christmas and the Advent season which precedes it (Reading 2.12).

The powerful words of Isaiah (Reading 2.13) can also apply to periods of darkness in our personal and spiritual lives, while Reading 2.14 provides the antidote, urging us to show some courage, raise our heads and look around to see the light has arrived rather than remaining in gloom. Finally, in one of the typical first-person statements about Jesus' identity to be found in the fourth gospel (Reading 2.15), Jesus describes his mission as dispelling the darkness and spreading light (or, to use another term based on a metaphor involving light, en*light*enment).

Q *Are you still groping around in the darkness? Is it possible that the light has arrived in your life but you just have not recognised it?*

Reading 2.12
The true light
What has come into being with him was life, and the life was the light of all people. The light *shines* in the darkness, and the darkness did not overcome it. The true light, which enlightens everyone, was coming into the world. *Jn 1:3–5, 9*

Reading 2.13
Darkness at noon
Justice is far from us and righteousness does not reach us; we wait for light, and lo! there is darkness; and for brightness, but *we walk in gloom*.

We grope like the blind along a wall … We stumble at noon as in the twilight … We wait for justice, but there is none, for salvation, but it is far from us. *Isa 59:9–11*

Reading 2.14
Look around you
Arise, shine, for your light has come and the glory of the Lord has risen upon you. For darkness shall cover the earth and thick darkness the peoples: but the Lord will arise upon you, and his glory appear over you. Nations shall come to your light, and kings to the brightness of your dawn. *Lift up your eyes* and look around. *Isa 60:1*

Reading 2.15
Light and Darkness
Then *Jesus cried aloud*: 'Whoever believes in me believes not in me but in him who sent me. And whoever sees me sees him who sent me. I have come as light into the world, so that everyone who believes in me should not remain in the darkness. I do not judge anyone who hears my words and does not keep them, for I came not to judge the world, but to save the world.' *Jn 12:44–47*

Q *Are you still groping around in the darkness? Is it possible that the light has arrived in your life but you just have not recognised it?*

(d) Incarnation: Overview

For an overview of the incarnation, you can now read all of this very dense passage (Reading 2.16). Having examined its key content in detail in the previous pages, you will be able to consider it in context. Note that it begins with the same words as the opening verses of the Old Testament.

Reading 2.16
Prologue to St John's gospel
In the beginning was the Word, and the Word was with God, and the Word was God. He was in the beginning with God. All things came into being through him, and without him not one thing came into being. What has come into being with him was life, and the life was the light of all people. The light shines in the darkness, and the darkness did not overcome it.

There was a man sent from God, whose name was John*. He came as a witness to testify to the light, so that all might believe through him. He himself was not the light, but he came to testify to the light. The true light, which enlightens everyone, was coming into the world.

He** was in the world, and the world came into being through him; yet the world did not know him. He came to what was his own, and his own people do not accept him. *But to all who received*

---

* John the Baptist, not the author of the gospel.
** Confusingly, 'he' refers to John the Baptist in the second paragraph but to the Word (Jesus) in the third.

him, who believed in his name, he gave the power to become children of God, who were born, not of blood or of the will of the flesh or of the will of man, but of God. And the Word became flesh and lived among us, and we have seen his glory, the glory as of a father's only son, full of grace and truth. From his fullness we have all received, grace upon grace. The Law indeed was given through Moses; grace and truth came through Jesus Christ. No one has ever seen God. It is the Father's only Son, who is close to the Father, who has made him known. *Jn 1:1–18*

This is the background John wants you, the reader, to bear in mind as you read his gospel. It contains his view of Jesus' identity and it repays careful reading. That this passage of eighteen verses has served as a starting point for considering the incarnation and in particular the Word made flesh, the Only Son and Jesus as the Light of the World demonstrates how rich it is. And there is yet more to note: the section in bold connects with Reading 2.11, and the idea that we can all become children of God if we, unlike his people, accept him and believe in him.

See also the opening section ('Old Testament imagery') of this chapter about the influence of Wisdom literature on John's image of the Word, which (or who) is described as being with God *in the beginning*, that is to say, to have been already in existence at the creation, indeed as being himself God. This is the Word that has become flesh in Jesus, the Son of the Father. Here is the basis for the insight and doctrine of God as a Trinity: Father, Son and Holy Spirit.

Gospel references
Mk 3:11; 14:61–62
Jn 1:1–18; 10:30, 36–37; 12:44–47

Chapter Three

Messiah

Peter said: 'You have the words of eternal life. We have come to believe and to know that you are the holy one of God.' Jn 6:68–69
Central to Jesus' identity is the fact that he is a faithful Jew, so when he is ready to launch his mission it is appropriate that he does so at the synagogue in his home town. Imagine his feelings as he steps up to speak in front of his neighbours in these familiar surroundings. Their reaction is one of astonishment as well as resentment or jealousy on the part of some:

> 'Where did this man get this wisdom and these deeds of power? Is not this the carpenter's son? Is not his mother called Mary?' … And he did not do many deeds of power there, because of their unbelief (Mt 13:54–55, 58).

The sentiments expressed by sceptical members of his home town congregation are not all that far from the social and intellectual snobbery Jesus encounters later when teaching in the Temple: 'How did he learn to read? He has not been educated' (Jn 7:25).

The words of Peter at the top of this page reflect the eventual conviction of his disciples that Jesus was the Messiah, the hoped-for deliverer of the Jewish people. Once the Messiah had established his rule, it was expected that an age of peace would dawn, anticipated in the idyllic but vague terms of a prophecy from Isaiah:

> The spirit of the Lord shall rest on him,
> the spirit of wisdom and understanding,
> the spirit of counsel and might,
> the spirit of knowledge and fear of the Lord …
>
> The wolf shall live with the lamb,
> the leopard shall lie down with the kid,
> the calf and the lion … together. *Isa 11:2, 6–7*

Jesus conceives his mission as bringing his message first to 'the lost sheep of the house of Israel' (Mt 10:6). However, he also heals gentiles and tells the Samaritan woman he meets at a well that the present arrangements will not last, and that the moment of breakthrough, the 'hour', is now, referring to his ministry and the coming of the kingdom. He qualifies the exclusivity of Jewish worship, 'Salvation comes from the Jews … but the hour is coming, *and is now here*, when the true worshippers will worship the Father in spirit and in truth', that is, rather than separately as Samaritans and Jews (Jn 4:23). Similarly, after remarking upon the gentile centurion's great faith, he uses the traditional image of a messianic banquet to suggest that gentiles too could enter into the heritage of Israel: 'I tell you, many will come from east and west and will eat with Abraham and Isaac and Jacob in the kingdom of heaven'(Mt 8:11).

The significance of the title

The Hebrew word Messiah means 'anointed one', as does the Greek *Christos* which in turn has given us the English *Christ*, so Jesus Christ is not a name but a title: Jesus the Messiah. Kings were anointed and it was accepted that the messiah would be of the lineage of King David (hence the alternative term 'Son of David'), although his exact nature and that of his future intervention in Jewish history was disputed. Some wanted or expected a mighty king or military conqueror, others a more spiritual leader, others still a combination of both, but in all cases intense hope was invested in his expected coming, a measure of the suffering of the Jewish people, living in a small country in a region dominated successively by great empires. Because of the disagreements about the Messiah, Jesus is reluctant to claim the title, telling his disciples not to talk about it, and he is ambiguous when asked directly about it. As it is, he has to escape from enthusiastic crowds who want to proclaim him king (Jn 6:15).

Once in the hands of his enemies and facing death, Jesus is free to acknowledge his identity and does so, but more directly in some versions than in others. When asked at his interrogation by the High Priest whether he is the Messiah, Jesus replies that he is, according to Mark (Mk 14:62), while in Luke he is asked whether he is the Son of God and answers 'You say that I am', which is correctly taken to amount to a cautious 'yes' (Lk 22:70). And when the Roman governor, Pontius Pilate, asks him insistently whether he is the King of the Jews, his answer in John is that he is indeed a king but that his kingdom is not of this world, while in Luke and Matthew it is the indirect non-denial 'You say so' (see Jn 19:36 and Lk 23:3, Mt 27:11). These are typical examples of how the parallel texts of the various gospels can vary in relatively minor ways, which nonetheless does at times result in definite differences in emphasis.

A charge of blasphemy was solely a matter for the Jews and a matter of indifference to the Romans who would have regarded disputes about the messiah as yet more evidence of how uniquely difficult a people they were. Any hint of political activity, on the other hand, would provoke a very different reaction, particularly at a time of significant unrest. This is why the religious authorities accuse Jesus of wanting or claiming to be King of the Jews and attempt to throw doubt on his political loyalty, continually trying to trip him up with questions such as whether it was lawful for Jews to pay taxes to the Romans, a controversial matter. He is quick-witted enough to get out of that particular trap by pointing out the emperor's head on a coin: 'Give to the emperor what is the emperor's and to God what is God's' (Mt 22:21). Nonetheless their strategy works in the end and Jesus is executed by the Romans, using their particularly cruel method, crucifixion.

> Then the assembly rose as a body and brought Jesus before Pilate. They began to accuse him, saying, 'We found this man perverting our nation, forbidding us to pay taxes to the emperor, and saying that he is himself the Messiah, a king' (Lk 23:1–2).

So when in the early days of his ministry the disciples of the imprisoned (and soon to be executed) John the Baptist come to Jesus and carefully enquire whether he is indeed 'the one who is to come', his response is understandably cautious and indirect, but clear enough to those familiar with the scriptures. He tells them to 'Go back and tell John what you hear and see; the blind see again, and the lame walk, lepers are cleansed, and the deaf hear and the dead are raised to life and the good news is proclaimed to the poor' (Mt 11:3–5).

This question seems to imply doubts about Jesus on the Baptist's part. Jesus' reply refers to texts in Isaiah generally considered to be about signs of the Messiah. He reads from and refers to one of them in the synagogue at Nazareth. The account of this first public appearance after his baptism (Reading 3.1) incidentally underlines both the importance of social justice, in the quotation from Isaiah (see also Reading 11.1), with its expectations about the Messiah, as well as the central role of Old Testament prophecy in the New Testament. We can also sense something of Jesus' commanding presence in Luke's account:

Reading 3.1
Prophecy fulfilled
When he came to Nazareth, where he had been brought up, he went to the synagogue on the Sabbath day, as was his custom. He stood up to read, and the scroll of the prophet Isaiah was given to him. He unrolled the scroll and found the place that it was written:

> The spirit of the Lord is upon me, because he has anointed me to *bring good news* to the poor. He has sent me to proclaim release to captives and to the blind sight, to set the downtrodden free. He then rolled up the scroll, gave it back to the assistant and sat down. All eyes in the synagogue were fixed on him. Then he began to speak to them, 'This text is being fulfilled today, even as you listen.' *Lk 4:16–21*

Visualise Jesus reading the text, putting yourself in the congregation. What impression does he make on you?

A direct challenge
Much later, there is one occasion when Jesus is far from cautious and acts publicly in a way which he must realise will attract attention and leave him open to accusations of political activity (Reading 3.2). When he arrives in Jerusalem from Galilee, he has already predicted his death and is in hiding in the knowledge that the authorities are spying on him and are likely to take action against him at any time. His symbolic entry into the city as a peaceful and humble messiah seated on a donkey earlier that day

(or the day before, according to one version) makes an early move against him unavoidable. He is greeted on that occasion by crowds shouting 'Hosanna to the Son of David!', hailing him as the messiah (Mt 21:9). Later, children repeat the cry within the Temple precincts to the great irritation of the chief priests (Mt 21:15). His disciples had gone so far as to shout 'Blessed is the king who comes in the name of the Lord!' (Lk 19:38) The use of the word 'King' would be of interest to the Romans, as is demonstrated in the interrogation by Pontius Pilate after his arrest, when, as we have seen, he specifically asks Jesus whether he is the King of the Jews. The notice of his crime put above him on the cross reads: 'Jesus of Nazareth, King of the Jews' (Jn 19:19).

To return to the events after Jesus' entry into Jerusalem: before his next public act, Jesus weeps over the city's failure to 'recognise the time of your visitation from God', an interesting choice of words (Lk 19:41–44). He then does something deeply symbolic which can only be seen as deliberately and openly challenging the religious authorities: he goes into the Temple, the centre of the Jewish religion, and drives out the money-changers and stallholders. It comes at a time when the authorities are determined to arrest him but are nervous to do so in a city crowded with pilgrims about to celebrate Passover. Even after the demonstration on his entry into Jerusalem and his clearing of the Temple he continues to teach large and enthusiastic crowds and to heal there openly (Lk 19:47 and Mt 21:14), while the chief priests have already taken up his blatant challenge and are actively preparing to silence him permanently at the earliest opportunity. As it is, their task is made much easier by Judas' betrayal of Jesus to the authorities (Mt 26:14).

The chief priests and the Pharisees, not natural allies, had already summoned a meeting of the Council, the Jewish civil authority, to decide how to deal with Jesus.

> 'If we let him go on like this, everyone will believe in him, and the Romans will come and destroy both our holy place and our nation.' But one of them, Caiaphas, who was high priest that year, said to them … 'You do not understand that it is better for you to have one man die for the people than to have the whole nation destroyed' … So from that day on they planned to put him to death. *Jn 11:48–50*

At Jesus' trial a short time later, some witnesses claim to have heard him say he would destroy the Temple and build another within three days (Mk 14:58). A remark he makes as he and the disciples are leaving the Temple where the crowd has been listening 'with delight' (Mk 12:37) to his condemnation of the scribes, lies behind the testimony: 'Not one stone will be left here upon another: all will be thrown down' (Mk 13:2). While the authors of the other two synoptic gospels had the example of the destruction of the Temple by the Romans in AD 70 in mind when writing up the sayings of Jesus, Mark probably was writing before that happened. It is probably a symbolic reference to replacing the current religious leadership centred on the Temple with something based on the values of the kingdom of God. As things turned out, the Temple and the priesthood were already in the last few decades of their existence, as they were not to survive the disaster of the crushing military defeat of AD 70 and its aftermath, and have never been restored since.

Continuing the symbolism of buildings, and following on from his words about the Temple, the gospels have Jesus applying Psalm 117 to himself at this point. It testifies to his confidence in the challenge he is making to those who hold religious and political power in his country, despite the certainty of his death:

> The stone that the builders rejected
> has become the corner-stone;
> this was the Lord's doing,
> and it is amazing in our eyes. *Mk 12:10–11*

Reading 3.3, known as the allegory of the vineyard, is told by Jesus immediately after these dramatic events in Jerusalem. It tells the story of the repeated rejection of the prophets sent by God. The final representative he sends is his son, who is murdered. The answer to Jesus' closing question is obvious enough to those listening: after punishing the existing tenants, the landlord in the story will find new tenants who will give him the produce after the harvest. This refers to a new covenant with a new Israel made up of some Jews and extended to Gentiles. It places Jesus in the lineage of the prophets and, significantly, it identifies him as the Son. It also accepts, despite the crowds who listen to his preaching, that he has failed to convert the great mass of the people, certainly in Jerusalem. Finally, Mark makes it clear that the Temple authorities understand only too well the implications of Jesus' harsh words in the allegory of the vineyard. They want to arrest him immediately, but fearing the reaction of the crowd, leave him alone for the moment (Mk 12:12).

Reading 3.2
Cleansing the Temple
The crowds that went ahead of him and that followed were shouting, 'Hosanna to the son of David! Blessed is the one who comes in the name of the Lord! Hosanna in the highest heaven!' When he entered Jerusalem, the whole city was in turmoil, asking, 'Who is this?' The crowds were saying, 'This is the prophet Jesus from Nazareth in Galilee.' Then Jesus entered the Temple and drove out all who were selling and buying … and he overturned the tables of the money-changers and the seats of those who sold doves. He said to them 'It is written "My house shall be called a *house of prayer*" but you are making it a den of robbers.' *Mt 21:9–13*

We get a clear idea of how Jesus understood his identity in this context from the story he tells shortly after the momentous events described in the two previous readings. A vineyard is a recognised symbol of Israel.

Reading 3.3
The vineyard
'There was a landowner who planted a vineyard, put a fence around it, dug a wine press in it, and built a watchtower. Then he leased it to tenants and went to another country. When the harvest time had come, he sent his slaves to the tenants to collect his produce. But the tenants seized his slaves and beat one, killed another, and stoned another. Again he sent other slaves, more than the first; and they treated them in the same way. Finally he sent his son to them, saying, 'They will *respect* my son.' But when the tenants saw the son, they said to themselves, 'This is the heir; come, let us kill him and get his inheritance.' So they seized him, threw him out of the vineyard, and killed him. Now when the owner of the vineyard comes, what will he do to those tenants?' *Mt 21:33–40*

Gospel references
Mt 8:11; 10:6; 13:54–58; 21:8–16; 22:15–21; 27:11
Mk 11:15–18; 12:1–12; 14:58, 61-62, 66-7
Lk 19:37–38; 22:70; 23:1–3
Jn 4:21–24; 6:15, 68–69; 18:33–38

Chapter Four

Healer

As the sun was setting, all those who had any who were sick with various kinds of diseases brought them to him; and he laid his hands on each of them and cured them. Lk 4:40

It is easy to overlook the important part played by healing in Jesus' ministry. He heals what we would now call psychological and spiritual conditions as well as physical illness or disability. What is striking about the many healings described in the gospels is that Jesus typically congratulates the healed person (or whoever is asking for help on their behalf) on their faith, as in the first two Readings. Indeed this is the commonest context in which faith is mentioned in the gospels. Similarly, lack of faith on the part of the sick and afflicted and those who care for them means that healing is difficult or impossible: 'And he did not do many deeds of power there because of their unbelief' (Mt 13:58). Faith, in these accounts of Jesus' healings, means believing in him rather than believing that some aspect of his teaching is true.

Healing depends then on an act of faith in Jesus. It is the leper confidently telling him, indeed almost challenging him, that he is sure he can be healed: 'Lord, if you choose you can make me clean' (Mk 1:40); or the centurion who is certain that Jesus can cure his servant at a distance: 'Only speak the word and my servant will be healed.' He remarks of this gentile soldier that he has not found such faith in anyone in Israel (Mt 8:5–13). The woman in Reading 4.2 says to herself, 'If I can but touch his clothes, I will be made well.' All three of them demonstrate their faith in Jesus and, it is worth noting, and it is surely no accident, all are members of groups considered 'unclean'. Jesus touches the leper, for example, a gesture of acceptance towards somebody who was totally excluded from normal society and viewed with disgust:

'Moved with pity, Jesus stretched out his hand and touched him … Immediately the leprosy left him and he was made clean' (Mk 1:41–42).

At the same time, accounts of healing can have symbolic value, becoming narrative metaphors: healing blindness through faith in Jesus does not need much explaining. Nor does the blind man being called and after the cure following Jesus and the disciples along the road. Note also how his persistence in calling upon Jesus is rewarded (Reading 4.1), a feature of Jesus' teaching about prayer as illustrated by the humorous parable of the judge and the widow who pesters him mercilessly until he hears her case (Mt 18:1–5).

In Reading 4.2 the woman suffering from a haemorrhage is convinced that if she can only touch Jesus' clothing anonymously as he passes by in the crowd her shaming condition will be discreetly cured. She is distraught when Jesus asks who touched him, but he addresses her affectionately: 'Daughter, your faith has made you well.' This moving story is just one example of Jesus' gracious behaviour towards women. He treats them with respect and clearly does not regard their physicality as a sign of inferiority or uncleanness.

Reading 4.3 is a different sort of healing story. In this case it is Jesus who takes the initiative rather than responding to a request. Taking pity on the woman, he calls her over and promptly cures her. The complication is that it is in the synagogue on the Sabbath. The leader of the synagogue's harsh words prompt Jesus to speak severely in return. In this story, he is a figure of sovereign authority both as a healer and as a teacher. He considers himself empowered to ignore strict interpretations of the Sabbath restrictions if it is in order to achieve a greater good ('The Son of Man is Lord of the Sabbath', Mt 12:8). One can imagine the anger and outrage such an incident would cause in those who saw themselves as defenders of religion and good order. Just as he scandalously calls the tax collector Zacchaeus a son of Abraham (Reading 14.4), so Jesus refers to the woman as a daughter of Abraham, in effect insisting that for him, there were no excluded groups in Judaism or in the kingdom of God and that it included outcasts of all sorts, and both sexes equally.

Q *Are you able to make an act of faith? If so, in whom or what?*

Reading 4.1
'Your faith has made you well'
As he and his disciples and a large crowd were leaving Jericho, a blind beggar was sitting by the roadside. When he heard it was Jesus of Nazareth he began to shout out and say, 'Jesus, Son of David, have mercy on me!' Many sternly ordered him to be quiet, but he cried out even more loudly, 'Son of David, have mercy!' Jesus stood still and said 'Call him here.' And they called the blind man saying to him 'Take heart; get up, *he is calling you*.' So throwing off his cloak he sprang up and came to Jesus. Then Jesus said to him 'What do you want me to do for you?' The blind man said 'My teacher, let me see.' Jesus said to him, 'Go, your faith has made you well.' Immediately he regained his sight and *followed him* on the way. *Mk 10:46–52*

Reading 4.2
'Go in peace and be healed'
A large crowd followed him and pressed in on him. Now there was a woman who had been suffering from haemorrhages for twelve years. She had endured much under various physicians and had spent all her money but was no better; indeed she grew worse. She had heard about Jesus and came up behind him in the crowd and touched his cloak, for she said, 'If I can but touch his clothes, I will be made well.' Immediately her haemorrhage stopped; and she felt in her body that she was cured of her disease … Aware that power had gone forth from him, Jesus turned about in the crowd and said, 'Who touched my clothes?'… He looked all around to see who had done it. But the woman, who knew what had happened, came *in fear and trembling*, fell down before him and told him the whole truth. He said to her, 'Daughter, your faith has made you well; go in peace and be healed of your disease.' *Mk 4:24–34*

Reading 4.3
Healing on the Sabbath
He was teaching in one of the synagogues on the Sabbath. And just then there appeared a woman with a spirit that had crippled her for 18 years. She was bent over and was quite unable to stand up straight. When Jesus saw her, he called her over and said,

'Woman, you are set free from your ailment.' When he laid his hands on her, immediately she stood up straight and began praising God. The leader of the synagogue, indignant because Jesus had cured on the Sabbath, kept saying to the crowd, 'There are six days on which work ought to be done; come on those days to be cured, and not on the Sabbath day.' But the Lord answered him and said, 'You hypocrites! Does not each of you on the Sabbath untie his ox or his donkey from the manger, and lead it away to give it water? And ought not this woman, a daughter of Abraham whom Satan bound for 18 long years, be set free from this bondage on the Sabbath day?' When he said this, all his opponents were *put to shame*, and the entire crowd was rejoicing at all the wonderful things he was doing. *Lk 13:10–17*

Q *What are the implications for the sick of these three readings?*

Gospel references
Mt   8:1–5,14–16; 9:1–7; 12:8–13; 13:58; 15:29–31; 18:1–5
Mk   1:40–42

Chapter Five

Suffering Servant

'This is my blood of the new covenant.' Mt 26:28

'When I am lifted up from the earth, I will draw all people to myself' (Jn 12:32). These words of Jesus about the crucifixion puzzle his audience, although as with other veiled statements in the gospels, they will no doubt look back later, realising what he meant. He regards his death by now as both inevitable and necessary: 'Unless a grain falls into the earth and dies it remains just a single grain; but if it dies, it bears much fruit' (Jn 12:24). The thinking behind this statement is also present in John the Baptist's calling Jesus the Lamb of God: 'Here is the Lamb of God who takes away the sin of the world!' (Jn 1:29). The reference is to the sacrificial lamb of Passover (see the notes to Reading 7.1).

However, the clearest expression of the idea of Jesus' death as a sacrifice on behalf of others is to be found in a book written long before the events took place. It seems likely that, in his own understanding of his identity and mission, Jesus himself drew on Isaiah's imagery of the Servant of the Lord. Matthew quotes verses 1 and 2 from Isaiah 42 in the narrative section of his gospel (Mt 12:17–21): 'Here is my servant, whom I uphold, my chosen, in whom my soul delights; I have put my spirit upon him; he will bring forth justice to the nations' (Isa 42:1). A reference to the Servant of the Lord lies behind the words of God's endorsement of Jesus when he is baptised (see Preludes).

The Servant is probably in the first place a personification of Israel, but many saw in the text an additional reference to a mysterious individual. In later chapters (Isa 50:4ff and 52:13ff), Isaiah stresses the suffering of the Servant (Reading 5.1), actually using the image of a sacrificial lamb: 'He was oppressed and he was afflicted, yet he did not open his mouth; like a lamb that was led to the slaughter …' (Isa 53:7). This specific text is explained by Paul as a reference to Jesus when he is dealing with the questions of an Ethiopian interested in converting to Christianity (Acts 8:12–15). The verses of Isaiah, applied to the suffering and death of Jesus, have significantly affected the way these were (and still are) interpreted and portrayed:

Reading 5.1
For our transgressions

> Surely he has borne our infirmities
> and carried our diseases;
> yet we accounted him stricken,
> struck down by God and afflicted.
> But he was wounded for our transgression,
> crushed for our iniquities;
> upon him was the punishment that made us whole,
> and by his bruises we are healed.
> All we like sheep have gone *astray*;
> we have all turned to our own way,
> and the Lord has laid on him
> the iniquity of us all. *Isa 53:4–6*

You can see how these powerful verses came to be directly applied to Jesus and further developed in examples such as this one from the first letter of Peter:

> When he was abused, he did not return abuse; when he suffered, he did not threaten; but he entrusted himself to the one who judges justly. He himself *bore our sins in his body* on the cross, so that, free from sins, we might live for righteousness; *by his wounds you have been healed. For you were going astray like sheep,* but now you have returned to the shepherd and guardian of your souls. *1 Pet 2:23–25*

The Crucifixion
Regarding the crucifixion as an isolated event distorts it. While it is understandable that the various New Testament authors should try to find positive meaning in such an (apparent) disaster, the reader risks losing sight of the overall context if he or she concentrates exclusively or primarily on the cross. In this case the

context is the whole period of four days from the Last Supper on Thursday night to the risen Jesus standing among his followers in their hiding place the following Sunday evening. Viewed in that perspective, the crucifixion proves to be an important step on the way, not the final destination. In trying to make sense of it, the authors naturally turn to analogy and metaphor. In the view of the author of Hebrews, Jesus can be thought of as a heavenly high priest, who does not need to offer sacrifices daily for his own sins and those of others as 'This he did once and for all when he offered himself' (Heb 7:27); clear enough, though a rather clumsy analogy, if you think about it.

Paul argues that faith in Jesus Christ has replaced the Old Testament Law as a means of achieving forgiveness for sins and thus righteousness. We are justified (made righteous) he says 'through the redemption that is in Christ Jesus, whom God put forward as a sacrifice of atonement by his blood effective through faith'. (Rom 3:24–25). That sacrifices for sin were repeatedly offered under the old law, suggests, he claims, that they could not have been all that successful; as the author of Hebrews puts it, 'It is impossible for the blood of bulls and goats to take away sins' (Heb 10:4). On the other hand, Jesus 'offered for all time a single sacrifice for sins' (Heb 10:12), which was effective because '(God) forgave us all our trespasses, erasing the record that stood against us with its legal demands. He set it aside, nailing it to the cross' (Col 2:13–14).

The references to blood sacrifice here recall two central instances of animal sacrifice in the Judaism of New Testament times. Every year, on the Day of Atonement, when Jews call to mind their sins, the high priest, after sacrificing one goat, ritually transferred the sins of the whole nation on to another, the 'scapegoat', which was then released into the desert, taking its burden with it. Similarly, the Passover lamb was slaughtered every year and it should be remembered that the events around the first Easter coincided, or overlapped, with, Passover and that the Last Supper was either a Passover meal or took the form of one.

Much of the terminology used in these examples is problematic for people of our time. Metaphors of *atonement*, *redemption* and *blood sacrifice* all have roots in ancient society, whether in their legal systems (atonement, making good the damage done, as in the quotation from Colossians 2 a couple of paragraphs ago), in transactions such as buying a slave's freedom (redemption) or in religious rites such as that involving the scapegoat. *Ransom*, associated in our minds with the taking of hostages by terrorists, unfortunately remains meaningful: 'There is one mediator between God and humankind, Christ Jesus, himself human, who gave himself a ransom for all' (1 Tim 2:5–6), while the idea of *reconciliation* still works: 'In Christ God was reconciling the world to himself' (2 Cor 5:19).

Some of these analogies have inevitably lost much of their force and immediacy. They can even seem repugnant to modern readers, although we need to remember that Jesus himself used imagery of blood and sacrifice during the Last Supper (see Reading 7.1), and that the Eucharist recalls those words every time it is celebrated. In due course, these ideas would all contribute to the developed Christian doctrine of the atonement, which teaches that Christ died for our sins.

Seeing the crucifixion in the broader context does not, however, diminish its horror. More effective in a way than direct description is its anticipation through Jesus' eyes during the experience in the Garden of Gethsemane immediately after the Last Supper (Reading 5.2). This is one of the most moving passages in any of the gospels (the versions of Mark and Mathew are very similar). Jesus, in showing the natural emotions of somebody about to undergo a terrible death, demonstrates that being Son of God does not detract from his humanity. That humanity is confirmed by the fear and loneliness he expresses at the prospect of his arrest and what he knows will follow it. He even asks to be spared if possible, but accepts the will of the Father. Here, for once, the theological point of an episode coincides with its psychological interest and we do get a real sense of Jesus' feelings at this crisis point. The resulting account of the experience certainly merits its traditional name of The Agony in the Garden.

Reading 5.2
'I am deeply grieved'
Then Jesus went with them to a place called Gethsemane; and he said to his disciples 'Sit here while I go over there and pray.' He

took with him Peter and the two sons of Zebedee*, and began to be grieved and agitated. Then he said to them, 'I am deeply grieved, even to death; remain here, and stay awake with me.' And going a little further, he threw himself on the ground and prayed, 'My Father, if it is possible, let this cup pass from me, yet not what I want but what you want.' Then he came to the disciples and found them sleeping; and he said to Peter, 'So, could you not stay awake with me one hour? Stay awake and pray that you may not come into the time of trial; *the spirit indeed is willing, but the flesh is weak.*' Again he went away for the second time and prayed, 'My Father, if this cannot pass unless I drink it, your will be done.' Again he came and found them sleeping, for their eyes were heavy. So leaving them again, he went away and prayed for the third time, saying the same words. Then again he came to the disciples and said to them, 'Are you still sleeping and taking your rest? See, the hour is at hand, and the Son of Man is betrayed into the hands of sinners. Get up, *let us be going.* See, my betrayer is at hand.' *Mt 26:36–46*

Gospel references
Mt 12:17–21
Jn 1:29; 12:24, 32

---

* James and John

Chapter Six

Risen Lord

Mary Magdalene went and announced to the disciples, 'I have seen the Lord.' Jn 20:18

The gospels suddenly seem to change gear when they approach the last days of Jesus' life. In the earlier chapters, indications of time, place and context are vague or conventional, as are the links between stories. Rather than true narrative, the text largely consists of freestanding episodes or artificially grouped sets of related sayings and stories by Jesus. From the Last Supper on, through Good Friday and into the first Easter Sunday the story is detailed and has a narrative drive which increases the sense of accelerating inevitability as Jesus is arrested, interrogated, tried and executed. Afterwards there is a pause filled with the emptiness and sadness of the tomb, followed by sudden wonder at the resurrection. The smooth progress of the narrative is then disturbed somewhat by divergences in the four accounts.

At the same time, the gospels present the resurrection in a noticeably restrained way, as a mystery rather than a miracle. In fact, if you read the four gospel accounts carefully, you will be surprised to see that they do not describe what happened at all, only its consequences for Jesus' followers:

1. The *empty tomb* as discovered in all three versions by Mary Magdalene (either alone or with some female companions), with the result that the first witnesses to the resurrection are women, testifying to their improved status compared to what it was in traditional Jewish society.
2. The *appearances to his disciples*. And in the gospels it is only to disciples, Jesus is not seen by anybody else.
3. The remarkable *change in their morale*. They go from a dispirited rabble which had scattered after Jesus' arrest, going into

hiding, to confident missionaries prepared to speak out publicly and suffer or even die for their faith a relatively short time
later. Something had happened to them which had trans-
formed everything.

Incidentally, when the women go to the senior apostles and
tell them of their amazing discovery, they are not believed, and
their testimony is condescendingly dismissed: 'These words
seemed to them an idle tale' (Lk 24:11). Given that it puts the male
disciples in an unfavourable light and in view of the low status
of female testimony in Judaism, it is highly likely that this is a re-
liable tradition. Its inclusion testifies to the fundamental honesty
of the evangelist, as well as to what unfortunately looks like the
sexism of the apostles.

Hesitation is also apparent in the variations in the detail of the
post-resurrection events as described in the gospels. There are
none in Mark, as the gospel ends suddenly and dramatically
when the women discover the empty tomb. The first two readings
in this chapter contain descriptions of three post-resurrection appearances by Jesus: one to Mary Magdalene alone, a second to
disciples on the road to Emmaus, and a third, to the 11 apostles.
See what you make of them. One thing you will notice: all three
indicate that the risen Jesus was not the same as he had been in
life.

Jesus appears to Mary Magdalene

John's account of the appearance to Mary Magdalene in the garden next to the tomb, remarkably enough the only appearance to
an individual described, rather than simply referred to, in the
gospels (and even more remarkably it is to a woman), confirms
that Jesus has changed in some fundamental way. Mary, his leading female disciple, whom he had healed and who knows him so
well, who has followed him faithfully from the earliest days in
Galilee (Lk 8:2), who does not go into hiding after his arrest, as
the male apostles do, who is faithfully present at the crucifixion
(Lk 23:49), and when he is taken down from the cross and laid in
the tomb (Lk 23:55), Mary does not recognise him now, even
when he speaks to her. Perhaps in her case she is all too convinced
of his death, having remained with him through his agony and
then accompanied his body to its resting place. What triggers

eventual recognition is that he calls her by name, but even then, when she naturally makes as if to embrace him, he tells her not to touch him.

Reading 6.1

Mary Magdalene at the tomb

She turned round and *saw Jesus* standing there but she did not know that it was Jesus. Jesus said to her 'Woman, why are you weeping? For whom are you looking?' Supposing him to be the gardener she said to him 'Sir, if you have carried him away, tell me where you have laid him and I will take him away.' Jesus said to her, 'Mary!' She turned and said to him in Hebrew 'Rabbouni!', which means teacher. Jesus said to her 'Do not hold on to me for I have not yet ascended to the Father.' *Jn 20:14–17*

The other appearances

The appearances of the risen Jesus are not part of some additional legend which developed over time. They are central to the preaching about Jesus Christ from the very beginning of the church's missionary activity, as we see in the Acts of the Apostles (for example Acts 13:30–31; 17:31). Saint Paul makes it clear in his letter to the Corinthians, referring to the time of his conversion just a few years after the resurrection and well before the gospels were written: 'I handed on to you ... *what I in turn had received*: that Christ died for our sins in accordance with the scriptures, and that he was buried, and that he was raised on the third day in accordance with the scriptures, and then he appeared to Cephas (Peter), then to the twelve ...' (1 Cor 15:3–5).

In Reading 6.1 we saw what happens when Mary Magdalene meets the risen Jesus by the tomb. Similarly in the final scene of John's gospel the apostles fail to recognise Jesus: 'Just after daybreak, Jesus stood on the beach, but the disciples did not know that it was Jesus.' Like Mary Magdalene, they still do not realise who it is even when he speaks to them (Jn 21:4–7). Again, the gospel accounts do not try to hide the embarrassing fact. Matthew's version of the appearances even admits that, despite seeing him, the eleven did not all believe it was Jesus: 'When they saw him they worshipped him; but some doubted' (Mt 28:17), as does Luke's, with Jesus' question when he appears to the disciples, 'Why are you frightened and why do doubts arise in your hearts?'(Lk 24:38).

The gospels also honestly retain discrepancies about where the appearances took place, whether it was in Jerusalem or back in Galilee where it all began. The appearances are limited in time, ceasing when Jesus 'returns to the Father'. Soon afterwards, a new age opens when the Holy Spirit descends on the disciples as they launch the Christian church at Pentecost (Acts 2:1–11).

It is surely significant that the story, found in all four gospels, about Jesus walking on the water similarly has the disciples not recognising him at first (Mt 14:22–33 and parallel versions). That story too is about faith, Jesus gently rebuking Peter when initial enthusiasm and courage in following him into the waves give way to doubt and fear of drowning: 'You of little faith, why did you doubt?' (Mt 14:22), an advance reference perhaps, to his threefold denial of Jesus when questioned by bystanders during his Master's interrogation (Mt 26:66–75).

On the Road to Emmaus

It is the first Easter Sunday. Two of his disciples meet Jesus while walking on the road to Emmaus and talk with him at length without recognising him. Ironically, they tell him about the amazing events of that day and listen as he explains the scriptures to demonstrate that what has happened had been foretold by the prophets. Throughout they remain unaware that they are talking to the same Jesus. They eventually go to an inn with him and it is only when he breaks bread and pronounces a blessing that they realise who it is. Confirming that he has changed and has not simply returned to pick up his life as it was before, he then disappears, just as he later suddenly appears, despite locked doors, among the gathered apostles (Lk 24:36; Jn 20:19).

In the prologue to St John's gospel, we read that the only Son (Jesus) 'makes known' the Father and here it is the act of pronouncing a blessing and breaking bread which makes him known. Like the Feeding of the Five Thousand (Mt 14:13–21), the story has been shaped by the church's (and therefore the author's) experience of the early form of the Eucharist or Holy Communion service, then as now the sacramental presence of the risen Jesus, and which, like this encounter with him, included lessons about the (Jewish) scriptures, and the breaking of bread (see Reading 7.1).

It is generally thought that chapter 21 of John's gospel is a postscript and certainly the closing item in chapter 20 does make a fitting finale to the immediate post-resurrection appearances in Jerusalem (although there is a final appearance in Galilee in the postscript). It is a week after Jesus' sudden, dramatic presence among the disciples and he returns to prove to Thomas, who had been absent that day and so had refused to believe, that he has risen. Thomas is convinced and his declaration of faith 'My Lord and my God!' would represent the climax of the gospel were it not for Jesus' reply, 'Blessed are those who have not seen and yet have come to believe' (Jn 20:29), which speaks directly to future believers.

Reading 6.2
The breaking of bread

When he was at the table with them, he took the bread, blessed and broke it, and gave it to them. Then their eyes were opened, and they recognised him; and he vanished from their sight ... That same hour they got to Jerusalem; and they found the eleven and the companions gathered together ... Then they told what had happened on the road, and how he had been *made known* to them in the breaking of the bread. While they were talking about this, Jesus himself stood among them and said to them, '*Peace be with you.*' They were startled and terrified and thought they were seeing a ghost. He said to them 'Why are you frightened and why are doubts arising in your hearts?' Lk 24:30, 31, 33, 35

When Jesus suddenly appears among his assembled followers, his greeting, as we saw, is to wish them all peace, the peace he had left with them on the eve of his death, now present in all their hearts:

Reading 6.3
Peace I leave you

'Peace I leave with you, *my peace* I give to you. I do not give to you as the world gives. Do not let your hearts be troubled, and do not let them be afraid.' Jn 14:27

Gospel references
Mt 14:13–21; 14:22–33; 26:66–75; 28:17
Lk 8:2; 22:54–62; 23:49; 24:11, 36–38, 50–52
Jn 20:19, 28–29; 21:4–7

Chapter Seven

Sacramental Presence

'Do this in remembrance of me.' Lk 22:19

Meals play a significant part in Judaism and feature prominently in the gospels, including in several of Jesus' parables (see for example Reading 9.1). Jesus is often portrayed at dinner as a guest of a great range of people, including tax collectors, a leper, even pharisees, as well as friends such as Lazarus and his sisters. He is no puritan when it comes to the pleasures of the table, indeed he is maliciously criticised for it: 'Look, a glutton and a drunkard, a friend of tax collectors and sinners!' (Mt 11:19). The Last Supper, on the evening of Jesus' arrest, the last of many meals with his disciples, was either an actual Passover meal or took the form of one, with its combination of prayer over the bread, breaking of bread, praise of God and drinking of wine. At the meal, Jesus anticipates his death, using the symbolism of the bread to refer to his body and the wine to the cup or blood of the new covenant (Reading 7.1). Paul here refers to what was already the practice of the Church when he became a follower of Jesus, not long after the first Easter.

Jesus clearly sees his impending death as in some way inaugurating the kingdom; looking forward to the symbolic messianic banquet he says: 'I tell you, I will never again drink of this fruit of the vine until the day when I drink it new with you in my father's kingdom' (Mt 26:29), another saying his disciples would understand better only after what was to happen on the following Sunday.

As the terrible events of Good Friday follow the Last Supper, the disciples are in shock, even though Jesus had warned them more than once of what was inevitably going to happen to him. They must also have felt desperately guilty at how they had reacted after his arrest: 'Then all the disciples deserted him and fled' (Mt

26:56). That bald statement gives them no room to hide. However, Easter transforms everything and in light of what they experience then, they will be able to look back on their final meal together as the beginning, and their regular celebration of what became Holy Communion as the continuation of the Lord's glorious triumph. They and the generations of his followers since have carried out his recorded wish that they do the same in memory of him.

At the Last Supper, Jesus also refers to a new covenant. The old covenant was the special relationship between the Jews and their God. Among others, the prophet Jeremiah had looked forward to a new covenant between God and the Jewish people. Rather than simply codify behaviour it would penetrate to the heart, the inner man and woman, (a common theme in both the Old and New Testaments, see Readings 2.2 to 2.6): 'I will put my law within them and I will write it on their hearts and I will be their God and they shall be my people' (Jer 31:32).

It was also recognised that a renewed covenant would have to be extended in some way and at some time to include gentiles. The fact is that the Jewish God had long been conceived as more than simply the deity of Israel. As he was the only God, even if the Jewish people enjoyed some special position in relation to him, the idea of a totally exclusive contract between him and a single people for all time came to seem increasingly untenable. This was complicated by the growing Christian church, despite becoming more gentile in its composition all the time, also seeing itself as the heir of Israel and fulfilling the prophecy of Isaiah: 'I will make you the light of the nations so that my salvation may reach to the ends of the earth' (Isa 49:6). Although Paul was proud of his Judaism and status as a Pharisee and, like the other disciples, continued to attend synagogue until forced out, he became convinced that gentiles could become full members of the originally Jewish church. Like Paul, although initially with much more hesitation, Peter too came to the conclusion that 'God shows no partiality, but in every nation anyone who fears him and does what is right is acceptable to him' (Acts 10:34). Hence the interpretation of Jesus' death as a sacrifice (of Jesus as the Passover Lamb of God) marking the beginning of a new covenant based on faith rather than the Jewish Law and which would indeed include gentiles.

In the fourth gospel Jesus' presence in the Eucharist gives eternal life, the equivalent of membership of the synoptics' kingdom of God, as well as communion with him: 'Anyone who does eat my flesh and drink my blood has eternal life. He ... lives in me and I live in him' (Jn 6:54, 56).

Reading 7.2 summarises the task ahead for his closest followers, who would become the leaders of the church. They are assured of Jesus' continuing presence until the world ends with the return of Christ in glory.

Reading 7.1
'This is my body'
For I received from the Lord what I also handed on to you, that the Lord Jesus on the night when he was betrayed took a loaf of bread and when he had given thanks, broke it and said 'This is my body that has been broken for you. Do this in remembrance of me.' In the same way he took the cup also, after supper, saying 'This cup is the new covenant in my blood. Do this, as often as you drink it, in *remembrance of me'* ... Whoever therefore eats the bread or drinks the cup of the Lord in an unworthy manner will be answerable for the body and blood of the Lord. Examine yourselves, and only then eat of the bread and drink of the cup. For all who eat and drink without discerning the Lord's body, eat and drink judgement against themselves. *1 Cor 11:23–29*

Reading 7.2
'I am with you'
'Where two or three are gathered in my name, I am there among them ... Go therefore and make disciples of all nations ... and remember, I am with you *always*, to the end of the age.' *Mt 18:20; 28:19–20*

Gospel references
Mt 11:18–19; 26:26–29, 56
Jn 6:52–58

PART TWO

THE TEACHING OF JESUS CHRIST

Part Two: Outline

Part Two: Introduction

Chapter Eight: Invitations
       8.1 Matthew 11:28–30
       8.2 Luke 5:27–32
       8.3 Revelation 3:20

Chapter Nine: The Kingdom
       9.1 John 5:24
       9.2 Luke 14:16–20
       9.3 Matthew 25:1–13
       9.4 Matthew 16:24

Chapter Ten: Authority
       10.1 Matthew 5:17, 21–24, 27–28 / Luke 6:27–30
       10.2 Luke 6:32–35
       10.3 Luke 6:43–45
       10.4 Matthew 7:24–29

Chapter Eleven: Social Justice
       11.1 Psalms 146:5ff
       11.2 Matthew 25:31–40
       11.3 James 2:14–17

Chapter Twelve: Forgiveness
       12.1 Luke 7:36–50
       12.2 John 8:3–11
       12.3 Luke 15:11–32

Chapter Thirteen: Humility and Simplicity
       13.1 Mark 10:35–45
       13.2 Luke 18:9–14
       13.3 Luke 18:15–17
       13.4 Matthew 11:25

Introduction

Whatever view one takes about the identity of Jesus Christ, the fact remains that his teaching, the product of a short ministry of at the most three years, has fascinated, inspired, and guided men and women throughout the twenty centuries that have passed since, despite the end of the world failing to arrive. The aim of this second part of the book is to allow Jesus to speak for himself. The Readings have been chosen to give a good idea of his ethical teaching in particular (which was always in the context of the coming of the kingdom of God) and of his distinctive voice. The idea behind Focused Reading is to enable you to listen to that voice.

It is a voice which speaks with *authority* (Reading 10.1), as well as being that of an accomplished *teacher* and *storyteller* (Readings 9.1, 11.2, 12.1, 12.3, 13.2, 16.2) with a gift for the *memorable* (and often humorous or surprising) *phrase*. Jesus prefers concrete examples drawn from everyday life to abstraction, such as knowing trees by their fruit as an analogy for judging people on what they do, and not on their status (Reading 9.3). In answer to the question as to why he frequents sinners, he replies that a doctor tends the sick, not the well (Reading 8.2), and rather than remark that you cannot reconcile membership of the kingdom of God with the pursuit of wealth, he says a slave cannot serve two masters (Reading 14.2). When he wants to stress generosity, he says if somebody takes your coat, give them your shirt, too (Reading 10.1).

What emerges from the teaching above all is his stress on *forgiveness* ahead of judgement, and his *openness* and acceptance of all, in particular those regarded as outside normal respectable society or as unclean, such as lepers (see Chapter 9 notes), tax collectors (Readings 9.2, 13.3, 14.4), or women in general (Readings 12.1, 12.2, see also 4.2). The other side of that coin is his fierce and courageous condemnation of the religious establishment, a further instance of his authority (see Chapters 8 and 10).

Jesus' teaching is *urgent*. There is a sense of crisis in the air and he is aware that he does not have long. In AD 66, just a generation later, the unstable mixture of ethnic, political and religious tensions already apparent as the background to the accounts of his ministry in the gospels would finally explode in a hopeless Jewish uprising brutally put down by the Romans. In response, by the time the last two gospels were written, the Romans had dismantled Jerusalem, including the Temple, and expelled its population. The world those gospels portray had vanished forever. Given the instability of the times, it is easy to understand the first couple of generations of Christians, whose experiences and beliefs are reflected in the synoptic Gospels, being convinced that the world would end relatively soon and that Jesus Christ would return in glory to judge all humankind. This is the dramatic context of Reading 11.2 (the Last Judgement).

However, in the tradition associated with the fourth gospel, probably written nearly half a century after Mark's gospel appeared, the lively expectation of a Second Coming had rather faded into the background. John continued to draw upon his different tradition with its distinctive emphases, but which nonetheless covers essentially the same ground as the synoptic gospels. For example, the decisive criterion in Matthew's detailed account of the Last Judgement is how one has treated the suffering, the unfortunate and the marginalised. Amounting to a radical call to love our neighbour, it is paralleled rather than replaced in John's gospel by a general but passionately felt call for love as a precondition to entering what is called 'eternal life', that is to say, the kingdom of God (see Readings 9.3 and 17.4).

One feature of Jesus' ethical teaching is that it has very little to say on the subject of sexual behaviour. Certainly, he warns against adultery in the heart in outlining his more stringent standard in which the inner disposition of the mind is taken into account in judging behaviour (Reading 10.1), and he includes adultery and fornication in the list of things which truly defile compared to breaches of the code relating to clean and unclean food. But that is all. And the one example of sexual sin with which he is confronted, the episode of the adulterous woman (Reading

12.2), is the occasion for one of his most surprising acts when he fails to condemn her because of the hypocrisy of her accusers. On the evidence of the gospels, Jesus did not give a central place to sexual sin. It is remarkable how that has been lost sight of.

Chapter Eight

Invitations

'If you continue in my word, you are truly my disciples; and you will know the truth and the truth will set you free.' Jn 8:32
The invitation in the first reading (8.1) is particularly relevant to the experience of men and women in our fragmented consumer society, in which, for the great majority, material needs are met but emotional, psychological and spiritual burdens are all the more keenly felt. You can read and reread this short passage and it never loses its charm and capacity to make you think about your life and priorities. In response to the text, try answering these questions after reflecting on it:

Q *In which ways does the Reading speak to you directly? Which particular 'burdens' came to your mind? What would 'rest for your soul' mean to you?*

The Pharisee yoke

The original contrast here is with the 'yoke' and burdens imposed by the Pharisees whose rigid insistence on the externals of religious observance constitutes, Jesus says, a barrier to ordinary people entering the kingdom of God. At the same time, in a devastating chapter of Matthew, in which he repeatedly calls them hypocrites who care more for status than the good of the people, he accuses the Pharisees of losing sight of what really matters by neglecting 'The weightier matters of the Law: justice and mercy and faith' (Mt 23:23). These are of greater significance as far as Jesus is concerned than observing the dietary laws or even keeping the Sabbath (see Reading 4.3). He also condemns the pharisees as blind guides of the blind: 'If one blind person guides another, both will fall into a pit' (Mt 15:14). This striking image has gone into our language as 'The blind leading the blind.'

Not all Pharisees deserved such total condemnation, and the hostility to them here partly reflects circumstances when the gospel was written, with an intense struggle going on between Jews who had become Christians and the synagogues who increasingly excluded them. They function as a sort of negative version of the values required to enter the kingdom of God. These opposing qualities can be paired off, with the Pharisees' negative characteristics first: the *letter* against the spirit; *exclusion* against openness and acceptance; *condemnation* against forgiveness and mercy; *status* against humility; *externals* against the heart. The negatives stand for an approach to religion and social morality which is not confined to history.

'Follow me!'

In Reading 8.2 the message could hardly be briefer. In fact, as is the case when he calls the apostles (Mt 4:18–22), it is brusque in its urgency: 'Follow me!' says Jesus to Levi the tax collector, who immediately rises from his desk, leaving everything behind. He then invites Jesus to be his dinner guest and he accepts. To the watching Pharisees, it was bad enough for Jesus to have included a tax collector among his followers, but accepting hospitality from one in the company of his friends was going too far. Tax collectors were despised and considered unclean, they acted on behalf of the gentile Roman occupiers and were regarded as little better than thieves as they earned their living by taking a cut of what they collected. When asked why he mixes with such people, Jesus sums up with a typically concrete everyday image rather than an abstract statement. Everyone can understand the point he is making, that doctors see to the sick, not the well.

Reading 8.3 is from the last book of the Bible, Revelation. This is a strange work full of dark symbolism, nonetheless it has some interesting passages which you could easily miss if you assumed it was all only about the end of the world. Here, Jesus is described as waiting outside the door for you to let him in. Open the door!

Reading 8.1
'Come to me!'
Come to me, all you that are weary and are carrying heavy burdens and *I will give you rest*. Take my yoke upon you, and learn from me; for I am gentle and humble in heart, and you will find rest for your souls. For my yoke is easy, and my burden is light. *Mt 11:28–30*

Reading 8.2
'Follow me!'
He went out and saw a tax collector named Levi sitting at the tax booth; and he said to him 'Follow me'. And he got up, *left everything*, and followed him. Then Levi gave a great banquet for him in his house; and there was a large crowd of tax collectors and others sitting at the table with them. The Pharisees and scribes complained to his disciples and said, 'Why do you eat and drink with tax collectors and sinners?' Jesus said to them in reply, 'It is not those who are well who need the doctor, but the sick. I have not come to call the virtuous, but sinners to repentance.' *Lk 5:27–32*

Visualise: Imagine yourself there. Without analysing what is happening, concentrate on the scene before you, take it all in. As the rabbi approaches, the noise of the crowd changes from a loud background murmur to an excited babble. You catch occasional glimpses of him through the crowd. He is heading towards you. You have seconds to decide what you are going to say when he invites you to follow him as a disciple.

Reading 8.3
Open the door
'Listen, I am standing at the door, knocking. If you hear my voice and open the door, I will come to you.' *Rev 3:20*

Gospel references
Mt 4:18–22; 15:14; 23:1–27

Chapter Nine

The Kingdom

Jesus came to Galilee, proclaiming the good news of God, and saying, 'The time is fulfilled and the kingdom of God has come near, repent and believe in the good news.' Mk 1:14–15

The Greek word translated as 'good news' in that quotation from Mark is also translated as 'gospel' elsewhere. That is what the Old English word 'godspel' means, so the words of Jesus could just as easily be 'believe in the gospel', which means the content of his preaching, his message. You can then see how the word came to be used for the books containing that message.

It is also a useful reminder that the version of the Bible we read or study can express the content in a different way from other versions. Find one that suits you or compare different versions if you find a passage puzzling or strangely expressed. To be literal-minded about the gospels is to pursue a mirage. After all, we are dealing with translations of translations in the case of the New Testament: Jesus spoke Aramaic, a daughter language of Hebrew, his sayings were eventually written down in Greek, the common language of the Mediterranean at the time, and we are using one particular English translation among many.

We could say, then, that the good news is that the kingdom of God has arrived, or is about to, and the gospel proclaimed by Jesus is that conversion is required if you are to enter it. In Readings 8.1 and 8.2 Jesus issues invitations to the kingdom of God, sometimes referred to in the gospels as the *kingdom of heaven* (to avoid using the sacred name) or *eternal life*. It is better translated as the kingship or reign of God and means living by God's rules. Jesus also speaks in terms of *metanoia* (usually translated as *conversion* or *repentance*) which literally means *new mind*, completely changing your mentality in order to be worthy of belonging to the kingdom.

Even though its full realisation is thought to lie in the future, the kingdom can come at any time: 'The kingdom of God is not coming with things that can be observed; nor will they say, "Look, here it is!" or "There it is!" For, in fact, the kingdom of God is among you' (Lk 17:20–21; the word translated *'among'* can also mean *'within'*). These words of Jesus amount to saying that the kingdom is already present, as he explains to the Samaritan woman in John 4:3 (see notes, Chapter 3). His words in the text of the gospel mean that it is potentially present now to its readers.

Despite being referred to as 'eternal life' in John's gospel, a term which can mislead, as it has acquired a more restricted meaning, there the kingdom is as much to do with this world as the next (Reading 9.1). It involves sharing in the life of the eternal God here and now through faith in Jesus his Son. In place of the expectation apparent in the three other gospels, and in Paul's earlier letters, of an early Second Coming of Jesus, the fourth gospel, which was written later than the others, focuses in particular on the coming descent of the Holy Spirit following Jesus' return to the Father. The assumption is that there will not (yet) be dramatic upheavals of the sort anticipated in the earlier gospels, rather a church to organise and lives to live (see Jn 14:15–17; 25–26; 16:4–15).

'Truly I tell you, the tax collectors and the prostitutes are going into the kingdom of God ahead of you' (Mt 21:31). Jesus' hard words to the Pharisees stress that the invitation to enter the kingdom is extended to all, including, or especially, repentant sinners, the marginalised and excluded. The religious establishment has had its chance. Jesus calls everyone without exception to repentance in the light of the coming of the kingdom. Many will change their approach to life as a result, others will go further and become disciples. A *disciple* (the Latin word for pupil or student) is a follower of a spiritual teacher (Hebrew: Rabbi). In the gospels, it usually refers to those more committed followers who leave home and family and literally follow Jesus on his mission. Among them are many women, a remarkable feature of his entourage (Lk 8:1–3).

The second Reading in this chapter is one of several parables about the kingdom of God involving banquets from which those invited or otherwise involved are absent or to which they are not admitted. This particular example also expresses Jesus' option for the poor and disadvantaged. Those originally invited make excuses when the time comes, so a servant is sent into the streets to bring in the poor and the sick instead.

Urgency and sacrifice

The parables of the kingdom stress above all the need for vigilance, and in particular they refer to its expected definitive arrival at the end of time, which could be very soon according to the synoptic gospels. In several of the parables, people are caught short by the arrival of a king or master. For example, the five bridesmaids refused entry to a wedding banquet because they have neglected to buy oil for their lamps and are buying some when the bridegroom arrives. They have missed their chance (Reading 9.3).

This teaching is characterised by the urgency we saw in his invitation to Levi the tax collector in Reading 8.2. There is a sense of an approaching dramatic climax, which will mark the beginning of a new age. See Mt 24:4–41, and Lk 21:8–36 for the two evangelists' accounts of what the expected end of the world would be like. Both were understandably influenced by the experience of the devastation which accompanied and followed the Jewish uprising eventually put down in AD 70. The 'kingdom of God is at hand' is an ambiguous expression which can refer to its arrival at a particular place or time or both (possibly very near and very soon).

Jesus makes clear that he expects his disciples to be ready for sacrifice in the service of the kingdom (Reading 9.4). Part of the price to be paid includes putting your family second: when told that his mother and brothers are outside, waiting to speak to him, he says, shockingly,

> 'Who is my mother and who are my brothers?' And, pointing to his disciples, he said, 'Here are my mother and my brothers. For whoever does the will of my Father in heaven is my brother and sister and mother.' (Mt 12:48–50).

Similarly, given the urgency of the situation and the likely outcome of his ministry, it comes as no surprise that he will not marry, although he does not insist on celibacy for his disciples, leaving it to individual choice,

For there are eunuchs who have been so from birth, and there are eunuchs who were made eunuchs by others, and there are eunuchs who made themselves eunuchs for the sake of the kingdom of heaven. Let anyone accept this who can (Mt 19:12).

Reading 9.1
Passing from death to life

Jesus said to them: 'Very truly I tell you, anyone who listens to my word and believes him who sent me *has eternal life*; and does not come under judgement, but has passed from death to life.' *Jn 5:24*

Reading 9.2
The banquet: a parable

Someone gave a great dinner and invited many. At the time for the dinner he sent his slave to say to those who had been invited, 'Come, for everything is ready now.' But they all alike began to make excuses. The first said to him: 'I have bought a piece of land, and I must go out and see it; please accept my apologies.' Another said 'I have bought five yoke of oxen and I am going to try them out; please accept my apologies.' Another said 'I have just been married, and therefore I cannot come.' So the slave returned and reported this to his master. Then the owner of the house became angry and said to his slave, 'Go out at once into the streets and lanes of the town and bring in *the poor, the crippled, the blind and the lame* … For I tell you, none of those who were invited will taste my dinner.' *Lk 14:16–20*

Reading 9.3
The parable of the ten bridesmaids

Then the kingdom of heaven will be like this. Ten bridesmaids took the lamps and went to meet the bridegroom. Five of them were foolish, and five were wise. When the foolish took their lamps, they took no oil with them; but the wise took flasks of oil with their lamps. As the bridegroom was delayed, all of them became drowsy and slept. But at midnight there was a shout, 'Look! Here is the bridegroom! Come out to meet him.' Then all those bridesmaids got up and trimmed their lamps. The foolish said to the wise, 'Give us some of your oil, for our lamps are going out.' But the wise replied, 'No! There will not be enough for you and for us; you had better go to the dealers and buy some for yourselves.' And while they went to buy it, the bridegroom came, and those who were ready went with him into the wedding banquet; and the door was shut. Later the other bridesmaids came also, saying 'Lord, Lord open to us.' But he replied, 'Truly I tell you, I do not know you.' *Keep awake therefore, for you know neither the day nor the hour. Mt 25:1–13*

Reading 9.4
Readiness for sacrifice
Then Jesus told his disciples, 'If any want to become my followers, let them deny themselves and *take up their cross* and follow me. For those who want to save their life will lose it, and those who lose their life for my sake will find it.' *Mt 16:24*

Gospel references
Mt 12:48–50; 19:12; 24:4–41
Lk 17:20–22; 21:8–36
Jn 4:23; 16:4–15

Chapter Ten

Authority

One day, as he was teaching the people in the temple … the chief priests and the scribes came with the elders and said to him, 'Tell us, by what authority are you doing these things? Who is it who gave you this authority?'
Lk 20:1–2

Read the whole of Matthew chapters 5–7 for the detail of the Sermon on the Mount, a collection of sayings which summarises Jesus' revolutionary teaching with its daring contrast between what people have been told hitherto and what he teaches. See also Reading 4.3 for a good example of his confident, commanding style in dealing with those in positions of formal authority. Reading 10.1 gives the flavour of the Sermon on the Mount from Matthew and the equivalent Sermon on the Plain in Luke, including examples of the rhetorical exaggeration typical of his teaching style.

Demonstrating his faith in Jesus' healing power, which he is confident will permit his sick servant to be treated at a distance, the Roman officer who comes to Jesus for help also, as a soldier, recognises natural authority when he sees it: 'For I am under authority myself, and have soldiers under me; and I say to one man: go, and he goes; to another, come here, and he comes; to my servant: do this, and he does it' (Mt 8:9).

People pay attention to what Jesus says. The immediate reaction of Levi the tax collector (Reading 8.2) to the invitation to follow him testifies to the rabbi's compelling personality and innate authority. However, his at times provocative behaviour and words have been noted. As the questions about his authority demonstrate (see the top of the page) the religious establishment is deeply suspicious of him. As with other questions designed to trap him into what could be interpreted as blasphemy or sedition, Jesus avoids giving a direct answer to these questions.

He outrages conventional religious opinion by fiercely denouncing the Pharisees, and openly criticising Sabbath, food and social taboos, unapologetically failing to observe them if there is a good reason. He heals on the Sabbath (Reading 4.3) and when it comes to food declares that we are not defiled by what goes into our mouths and stomachs but by what comes out of our hearts: 'Evil intentions, murder, adultery, fornication, theft, false witness, slander. These are what defile a person' (Mt 19:20). He declares sins forgiven and mixes with or seems to favour 'unclean' tax collectors, gentiles, lepers, prostitutes, outsiders, poor people and sinners and, to the astonishment even of his disciples, converses alone with women (Jn 4:27). You can hear the disapproval in the comment on his behaviour: 'This man ... welcomes sinners and eats with them' (Lk 15:2).

'But I say ...'
He is also not afraid to put forward on his own authority radical reinterpretations of the foundations of the Jewish religion, the Law (contained in the first five books of the Bible) and the writings of the prophets, explicitly contrasting his approach with the traditional interpretations. As with his views on 'unclean' food, he stresses the inner reality rather than outward conformity with rules. Even the commandments are treated in this way (see what he says about adultery and murder). His ethical teaching goes beyond the normal understanding of love of neighbour and embraces not only love of the stranger (Reading 11.1) or outsider (Reading 17.3) but even loving your enemy (Reading 10.1). In the second half of Reading 10.1 from Matthew and in the extract from Luke following it, he states his teaching in extreme terms to shake his audience and emphasise his point. Note also that reconciliation is placed above the formal requirements of religious practice: only when you have made your peace with your sister and brother are you entitled to ask something of God. Then in Reading 10.2 he spells out the principle behind his teaching, that we should in every sense give generously without expecting something in return.

Jesus is also impatient of those who judge others according to status, and instead puts forward a more concrete criterion: just as we know a tree by the fruit it produces, so we know somebody who is good by what they do, and the opposite (Reading 10.3). At the end of the Sermon on the Mount there is a typically concrete example of the authority which everyone sensed in him (Reading 10.4).

Reading 10.1
'I have come to fulfil the law and the prophets'
Do not think that I have come to abolish the Law or the prophets; I have come not to abolish but to fulfil ... You have heard that it was said to those of ancient times, you shall not murder ... But I say to you that if you are angry with a brother or sister, you will be liable to judgement. So when you are offering your gift at the altar, if you remember that your brother or sister has something against you, leave your gift there before the altar and go; first be *reconciled* to your brother or sister, and then, offer your gift ... It was said you shall not commit adultery. But I say to you that everyone who looks at a woman with lust has already committed adultery with her in his heart.

You have heard that it was said 'An eye for an eye and a tooth for a tooth.' But I say to you, do not resist an evildoer. But if anyone strikes you on the right cheek, turn the other one also ... and if anyone forces you to go one mile, go the other mile also. Give to everyone who begs from you, and do not refuse anyone who wants to borrow from you. *Mt 5:17, 21–24, 27–28*

And from the version of this teaching in the gospel of Luke:

> But I say to those that listen, love your enemies, do good to those who hate you, bless those who curse you, pray for those who abuse you ... and from anyone who takes away your coat, do not withhold even your shirt. *Lk 6:27–30*

Reading 10.2
Expect nothing in return
If you love those who love you, what credit is that to you? For even sinners love those who love them. If you do good to those who do good to you, what credit is that to you? For even sinners do the same. If you lend to those from whom you hope to receive, what credit is that to you? Even sinners lend to sinners, to receive as much again. But *love your enemies*, do good, and lend, expecting nothing in return. *Lk 6:32–35*

Reading 10.3
You recognise a tree by its fruit
No good tree bears bad fruit, nor again does a bad tree bear good fruit; for each tree is known by its own fruit. Figs are not gathered from thorns, nor are grapes picked from a bramble bush. The good person out of the good treasure of the heart produces good, and the evil person out of evil treasure produces evil; for it is out of the *abundance of the heart* that the mouth speaks. *Lk 6:43–45*

Reading 10.4
Founded on rock
Everyone who hears these words of mine and acts on them will be like a wise man who built his house on rock. The rain fell, the floods came, and the winds blew and beat on that house but it did not fall, because it had been founded on rock. And everyone who hears these words of mine and does not act on them, will be like a foolish man who built his house on sand. The rain fell, and the floods came, and the winds blew and beat against that house, and it fell – and great was its fall!' Now when Jesus had finished saying these things, the crowds were astounded at *his teaching*, for he taught as one having authority, and not as their scribes. *Mt 7:24–29*

Gospel references
Mt 5:1–7:29; 8:5–13; 15:17–20
Lk 6:17–46; 15:2
Jn 4:27

Chapter Eleven

Social Justice

Thus says the Lord: Maintain justice and do what is right. Isa 56.1
In Jewish teaching, religion and spirituality are always linked to ethical behaviour. It is not enough to be personally holy: righteousness has a social dimension. In Reading 11.1 the message is that those who act with compassion towards the unfortunate and the weak are doing the Lord's work, in effect acting as his agents.

In Reading 11.2, Jesus tells a story with a similar message about social justice and love of neighbour, including strangers. The criterion for judgement is whether we have shown compassion for the distressed and disadvantaged. This reading is less about the Last Judgement than it is about love of neighbour in the shape of the poor and unfortunate but the message is effectively underlined by that dramatic setting with all of humanity standing before the throne at the end of time.

Jesus gives a further twist to the teaching on social justice here: his story reverses the perspective of the previous reading from the psalms, where the Lord is seen to be helping the poor and oppressed through the righteous. In this case, they are surprised to learn that in encountering these various càtegories of unfortunate people from the margins of society, they were also encountering Jesus himself. So, according to this statement of solidarity, we meet or see him daily, whether in our own neighbourhood or on television, in the form of the sick and the starving, the homeless, the refugee, the drug user, the lonely and neglected, and the suffering. Given his identification with them, surely we can at least look upon them as brothers or sisters, however difficult that may be at times.

One of the classic disputes in Christian theology has been about the relationship between faith and what are called good works. However, in practical terms the answer is given by James: loving action is the sign of a living faith (Reading 11.3). 'Be doers of the word, and not merely hearers who deceive themselves' (Jas 1.22). James is making essentially the same point as Paul does in his eloquent praise of love above all other desirable qualities in a believer (Reading 16.3).

Reading 11.1
The Lord keeps faith forever

> Happy are those whose help is in the God of Jacob,
> whose hope is in the Lord their God ...
> who keeps faith for ever;
> who executes justice for the oppressed;
> who gives food to the hungry.
> The Lord sets the prisoners free;
> the Lord opens the eyes of the blind.
> The Lord lifts up those who are *bowed down*;
> the Lord loves the righteous.
> The Lord watches over the stranger;
> he upholds the orphan and the widow ...
> The Lord will reign forever, your God,
> O Zion, for all generations.
> Ps 146:5ff

Reading 11.2
'Lord, when was it we saw you?'
When the Son of Man comes in his glory ... All the nations will be gathered before him. Then the king will say to those at his right hand: 'Come ... inherit the kingdom prepared for you from the foundation of the world; for I was hungry and you gave me food, I was thirsty and you gave me something to drink, I was a stranger and you welcomed me, I was naked and you gave me clothing, I was sick and you took care of me, I was in prison and you visited me.' Then the righteous will answer, 'Lord when was it that we saw you hungry and gave you food, or thirsty and gave you something to drink? And when was it that we saw you a stranger and welcomed you or naked and gave you clothing?

And when was it we saw you sick or in prison and visited you?' And the King will answer them: 'Truly I tell you just as you did it to one of the least of these who are members of my family, *you did it to me.' Mt 25:31–40*

Q *What if that same criterion were applied to you?*
   Which other categories of people do you think would be mentioned if Jesus were telling the story today?

Reading 11.3
Putting faith into practice
What good is it if you say you have faith but do not have works? ... If *your brother or sister* is naked and lacks daily food, and one of you says to them, 'Go in peace; keep warm and eat your fill', and yet you do not supply their bodily needs, what is the good of that? So faith by itself, if it has no works, is dead. *Jas 2:14–17*

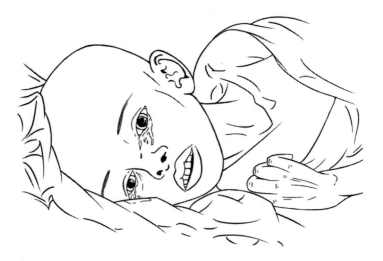

Chapter Twelve

Forgiveness

Be compassionate as your father is compassionate. Do not judge, and you will not be judged yourselves; do not condemn, and you will not be condemned. Lk 6:37

Forgiveness is at the heart of Jesus' teaching and ministry. We saw earlier how he stresses reconciliation in the Sermon on the Mount (Reading 10.1) and in the dramatic readings which follow we will discover just how radical his approach is.

The woman who was a sinner

Luke's gospel often portrays Jesus dining with others, including his opponents. He enjoys social occasions in all sorts of company. He is also notably at ease with women and has a large number of female followers (many of whom have, like Mary Magdalene, followed him throughout his ministry from the earliest days in Galilee), as well as female friends (Martha and Mary, the sisters of Lazarus). Here, he is relaxing in Simon the Pharisee's house, when a 'woman of ill repute' arrives, comes up to him weeping and kisses and anoints him, no doubt outraging the other guests. The act of anointing points ahead to his impending death: it will be women on their way to anoint his body who discover that the tomb is empty.

This gripping, beautifully written account is emotional and surprisingly physical. When the woman comes in, he allows her to touch him and kiss him. He is not embarrassed. Not only does he accept her attention, he does not hide the fact that he welcomes it. Her loving behaviour demonstrates that she has already been forgiven, he says, a surprising statement in itself. At this stage, he is careful not to say he forgives, or has forgiven, her sins: that is considered the prerogative of God and he knows he is being spied upon with a view to accusing him of blasphemy. His actions and words are bound to shock many present. Moreover, to them a woman touching the rabbi is bad enough, but such a woman, a known sinner. And anyway what gave Jesus the right to pronounce sins forgiven?

Recognising how offended Simon must be by the presence and actions of the woman, Jesus teases him, making light of her behaviour by humorously remarking on Simon's failure to show him the same consideration when he arrived at his house. He nonetheless reassures the woman before them all that her faith has saved her. Here, as in the accounts of healings carried out by Jesus, the faith that has saved her is concrete faith in him, not faith in a doctrine.

Reading 12.1
'She is a sinner'

One of the pharisees invited him to eat with him and he went into the Pharisee's house and took his place at the table. And a woman in the city, who was a sinner, having learned that he was eating in the Pharisee's house, brought an alabaster jar of ointment. She stood behind him at his feet, weeping, and began to bathe his feet with her tears, and to dry them with her hair. Then she continued kissing his feet and anointing them with the ointment. Now when the Pharisee who had invited him saw it, he said to himself 'If this man were a prophet, he would have known what kind of woman this is that is touching him, that she is a sinner.' Jesus spoke up and said 'Simon I have something to say to you … A certain creditor had two debtors: one owed 500 denarii, and the other 50. When they could not pay, he cancelled the debts for both of them. Now which of them will love him more?' Simon said 'I suppose the one for whom he cancelled the greater debt.' And Jesus said 'You have judged rightly.' Then turning towards the woman he said to Simon 'Do you see this woman? I entered your house; you gave me no water for my feet, but she has bathed my feet with her tears and dried them with her hair. You gave me no kiss, but from the time she came in she has not stopped kissing my feet. You did not anoint my head with oil, but she has anointed my feet with ointment. Therefore, I tell you that her sins, which were many, have been forgiven; hence she has shown great love. But the one to whom little is forgiven loves little.' Then he said to her 'Your sins are forgiven.' But those who were at the table with him began to say among themselves, 'Who is this who even forgives sins?' But Jesus said to the woman, *'Your faith has saved you; go in peace.'* Lk 7:36–50

Visualise: The room is crowded and noisy, all eyes on the guest of honour. When the woman enters and walks across the room towards him, silence falls on the gathering. What is she going to do? And what will Jesus do? Imagine yourself present, at the next table. Concentrate on the events you witness. How do others react? What strikes you about what she does? What strikes you about Jesus' response?

The adulterous woman

Reading 12.2 is just as gripping and surprising as the previous one and demonstrates once more the priority Jesus gives to mercy or forgiveness. Adultery was, and is, considered a very serious sin: it is specifically forbidden in the Ten Commandments and yet Jesus explicitly says he does not condemn the woman.

Although the death penalty for adultery was no longer in force in Jesus' day, in bringing the woman before him Jesus' enemies hope to put him in an impossible position: either to ignore the letter of the law and so seemingly condone what she has done, or to agree that the woman was indeed worthy of death and thereby damage his reputation as the friend of the sinner and the outcast. Jesus does neither. Before gently telling her to sin no more, he turns the sinfulness of the self-righteous group of men back on them and shames them so that they slink away embarrassed. You can imagine that once they have recovered their composure many of them will be angry.

Reading 12.2
'Neither do I condemn you'

The scribes and the Pharisees brought a woman who had been caught in adultery; and making her stand before all of them, they said to him, 'Teacher, this woman was caught in the very act of committing adultery. Now in the Law Moses commanded us to stone such women. Now what do you say?' They said this to test him, so that they might have some charge to bring against him. Jesus ... said, 'Let anyone among you who is without sin be the first to throw a stone at her ...' When they heard this they went away one by one, beginning with the elders; and Jesus was left alone with the woman standing before him. Jesus ... said, 'Woman, where are they? Has no one condemned you?' She said 'No one, Sir.' And Jesus said '*Neither do I condemn you.* Go on your way and from now on do not sin again.' *Jn 8:3–11*

Q *On the basis of these last two readings, what is Jesus' attitude to sin and sinners? Does it surprise you and if so, exactly how?*

The prodigal son
'But we had to celebrate and rejoice because this brother of yours was dead and has come to life; he was lost and has been found.' Central to this parable is a profound and moving sense of what it means to be a parent. God, too, is a loving Father. As with the adulterous woman in the previous reading, Jesus teaches that what he wants from a repentant sinner is a resolution to sin no more. Once this is apparent, forgiveness is always readily available. The same principle applies to people in their dealings with one another, as we saw in Reading 10.1.

The really interesting figure in the story is the other son who loyally stays with the father and works hard on the farm only to see his selfish younger brother welcomed with open arms. This is what makes the parable more than just a story with a moral and the characters more than stereotypes or abstractions. It makes us realise concretely how radical Jesus' teaching on forgiveness and reconciliation is.

Reading 12.3
A parable about forgiveness
There was a man who had two sons. The younger of them said to his father 'Father, give me the share of the property that will belong to me.' So he divided his property between them. A few days later the younger son gathered all he had and travelled to a distant country, and there he squandered his property in dissolute living. When he had spent everything, a severe famine took place throughout the country and he began to be in need. So he went

to work for one of the citizens of that country and was sent into his fields to feed the pigs. He would gladly have filled himself with the pods that the pigs were eating; and no one gave him anything.

When he came to himself he said, 'How many of my father's hired hands have bread enough and to spare, but here I am dying of hunger! *I will get up and go to my father*, and I will say to him "Father, I have sinned against heaven and before you; I am no longer worthy to be called your son; treat me like one of your hired hands."' So he set off and went to his father. But while he was still far off, his father saw him and was filled with compassion; he ran and put his arms around him and kissed him ... The father said to his slaves 'Quickly, bring out a robe – the best one – and put it on him, put a ring on his finger and sandals on his feet. And get the fatted calf and kill it, let us eat and celebrate; for this son of mine was dead and is alive again; he was lost and is found!' And they began to celebrate.

Now his elder son was in the field and when he came and approached the house, he heard music and dancing ... He became angry and refused to go in. His father came out and began to plead with him. But he answered his father 'Listen! For all these years I have been working like a slave for you, and I have never disobeyed your command ... When this son of yours came back, who has devoured your property with prostitutes; you killed the fatted calf for him!' Then the father said to him 'Son, you are always with me and all that is mine is yours. But we had to celebrate and *rejoice* because this brother of yours was dead and has come to life; he was lost and has been found.' *Lk 15:11–32*

Q *Relate this story to the circumstances of your own life and experience: Have you ever failed to forgive and regretted it? Have you ever yearned for forgiveness from someone and not obtained it?*
   What do you think of the attitude taken by the brother who stayed with the father?

Gospel reference
Mt 11:19

Chapter Thirteen

Humility and Simplicity

I will look to the humble and contrite in spirit. Isa 66:2
Complacency, presumption and even arrogance can all too often characterise religious people and Jesus is frequently highly critical of them. Even the twelve apostles, Jesus' inner group of disciples, are not free of the spirit of self-importance and jealousy, squabbling among themselves about which of them is the greatest (Mk 9:25). James and John even ask Jesus to place each of them at his side in the kingdom of God (Mt 20:21), not realising what suffering that would entail. The other ten are angry when they hear this and Jesus has to remind them all that service is their goal, not status (Reading 13.1).

We saw earlier how the Pharisees arrogantly question Jesus' teaching because he is not educated. When the blind man in John's gospel goes to have his cure authenticated, they are not impressed and when the healed man responds to their sceptical questions by saying that if Jesus were not from God he would not have been able to do anything, their furious reply before they throw him out shows the depths of contempt they feel for those they regard as sinners: 'Are *you* trying to teach *us*?' (Jn 9:34: emphasis added). In Reading 13.2 Jesus yet again provocatively makes a tax collector the central character in his story. Here he sets him alongside a self-deceiving pious pharisee who carries out all his religious duties, is proud that he does not sin and is scornful of the tax collector.

In Reading 13.3 Jesus overrules his disciples and welcomes the children who have been brought to see him. He tells his audience they need to show some of the characteristic attitudes of small children if they are to enter the kingdom of God. In keeping with this perspective, Jesus refers to his followers as 'infants' (Reading 13.4).

Reading 13.1
Not to be served, but to serve
James and John, the sons of Zebedee, came forward to him and said to him, 'Teacher, we want you to do for us whatever we ask of you.' And he said to them, 'What is it you want me to do for you?' And they said to him, 'Grant us to sit, one at your right hand and one at your left, in your glory.' But Jesus said to them 'You do not know what you are asking. Are you able to drink the cup that I drink, or be baptised with the baptism that I am baptised with?' They replied, 'We are able.'

When the ten heard this, they began to be angry with James and John. So Jesus called them and said to them, 'You know that among the gentiles those whom they recognise as the rulers lord it over them, and the great ones are tyrants over them. But it is not so among you; whoever wishes to become great among you must be your servant, and whoever wishes to be first among you must be slave of all. For the Son of Man came not to be served but to serve ...' *Mk 10:35–45*

Reading 13.2
'Be merciful to me, a sinner!'
Jesus also told this parable to some who trusted in themselves that they were righteous and regarded others with contempt. 'Two men went up to the temple to pray, one a Pharisee and the other a tax collector. The Pharisee standing by himself was praying thus, "God, I thank you that I am not like other people: thieves, robbers, adulterers, or even like this tax collector. I fast twice a week; I give a tenth of all my income." But the tax collector, standing far off, would not even look up to heaven, but beating his breast and saying "God, be *merciful* to me, a sinner!" I tell you, this man went down to his home justified rather than the other; for all who exalt themselves will be humbled, but all who humble themselves will be exalted.' *Lk 18:9–14*

Reading 13.3
The kingdom of God belongs to such as these
People were bringing even infants to him that he might touch them; and when the disciples saw it they ordered them not to do it. But Jesus called for them and said 'Let the little children come

to me, and do not stop them; for it is to such as these that the kingdom of God belongs. Truly I tell you, whoever does not receive the kingdom of God as a little child will never enter it.'
Lk 18:15–17

Reading 13.4
Hidden from the wise
Jesus said 'I thank you, Lord of heaven and earth, because you have hidden these things from the wise and intelligent and have *revealed* them to infants.' *Mt 11:25*

Q *Which specific qualities of a baby or young child do you think Jesus has in mind in the last two Readings?*

Gospel references
Mt 11:19; 20:20–22
Mk 9:25; 9:33–37
Jn 9:34

Chapter Fourteen

Money

Be on your guard against all kinds of greed; for one's life does not consist in the abundance of possessions. Lk 12:15

Jesus' teaching here is quite clear and explicit, although many have tried to soften or reinterpret it: you cannot serve God and money. In this matter the priorities of the kingdom of God are simply not those of the society around us. Jesus more than once warns of the dangers of wealth and its pursuit especially for those who wish to become disciples. Anyway, thinking that a great fortune will make you secure is a delusion, human life is short and the future uncertain.

In Reading 14.1 the rich man is sincere and no doubt fulfils his religious duties conscientiously but is nonetheless in for a shock. When asked what he must do to have eternal life (a synonym for entering the Kingdom of God), Jesus replies that if he wishes to go beyond keeping the commandments and become a disciple, that is join Jesus on the road, then he should sell all his possessions and give the proceeds to the poor. In Reading 14.2 he puts the same point in a striking image: you cannot serve two masters and so must choose between God and money. The consequences of applying that principle prove to be too much for the rich man to contemplate. Jesus is sympathetic but the principle stands, as he stresses at the end of the first Reading with one of his memorable rhetorical exaggerations. Reading 14.3 underlines the futility of amassing goods and wealth.

However there is an example in the gospels of a rich man successfully entering the kingdom. Zacchaeus is not only wealthy, he is also a senior tax collector, a member of a despised profession known for its thieving ways. In his enthusiasm to see Jesus, he climbs a tree and is still up the tree when Jesus passes by, stops and calls him by name, saying that he will dine at his house. This lively, vividly described, almost comic scene concludes with Zacchaeus publicly undertaking to more than make good what he has stolen in the past and give half of what he possesses to the poor. He has understood what is required (Reading 14.4).

Reading 14.1
He became sad
You know the commandments: 'You shall not commit adultery; you shall not murder; you shall not steal; you shall not bear false witness; honour your father and mother.' He replied, 'I have kept all these since my youth.' When Jesus heard this, he said to him, 'There is still one thing lacking. Sell all that you own and distribute the money to *the poor*, and you will have treasure in heaven; then come, follow me.' But when he heard this, *he became sad*; for he was very rich. Jesus looked at him and said, 'How hard it is for those who have wealth to enter the kingdom of God. Indeed, it is easier for a camel to go through the eye of a needle than for someone who is rich to enter the kingdom of God.' *Lk 18:20–25*

Reading 14.2
No one can serve two masters
Do not store up for yourselves treasures on earth, where moth and rust consume and where thieves break in and steal; but store up for yourselves treasures in heaven, where no moth consumes and where thieves do not break in and steal. For where your treasure is, *there your heart will be* also ... No one can serve two masters; for a slave will either hate the one and loathe the other, or be devoted to the one and despise the other. You cannot serve God and wealth. *Mt 6:19–21, 24*

Reading 14.3
Amassing wealth
Then he told them a parable: 'The land of a rich man produced abundantly. And he thought to himself, "What should I do, I have no place to store my crops?" Then he said, "I'll do this: I will pull down my barns and build larger ones to store my grain and my goods. And I will say to my soul, "You have ample goods laid up for many years; relax, eat, drink, be merry".' But God said to him,

'You fool! *This same night* your life is being demanded of you. And the things you have prepared, whose will they be?' So it is with those who store up treasures for themselves. *Lk 12:16–21*

Q   Where have you invested your 'treasure'?

Reading 14.4
'The Son of Man came to seek out the lost'
He entered Jericho and was passing through it. A man was there named Zacchaeus: he was a chief tax collector and was rich. He was trying to see who Jesus was, but on account of the crowd he could not because he was short of stature. So he ran ahead and climbed a sycamore tree to see him, because he was going to pass that way. When Jesus came to the place, he looked up and said, 'Zacchaeus, come down; for I must stay at your house today.' So he hurried down and was happy to welcome him. All who saw it began to grumble and said, 'He has gone to be the *guest* of one who is sinner.' Zacchaeus stood there and said to the Lord, 'Look, half of my possessions, Lord, I will give to the poor; and if I have defrauded anybody of anything I will pay back four times as much.' Then Jesus said to him, 'Today salvation has come to this house, because he too *is* a son of Abraham. For the Son of Man came to seek out and to save the lost.' *Lk 19:1–10*

By his actions, Zacchaeus proves that he has made the necessary and difficult choice between God's values and wealth. For disciples, however, the priorities of the kingdom are more demanding, whether it has to do with money and possessions, as in Reading 14.1, or family ties ('My mother and my brothers are those who hear the word of God and do it' *Lk 8:21*). In the next chapter, we consider some other priorities from the teaching of Jesus and of Paul, applying the teaching in concrete advice to early Christian congregations.

Gospel reference
Lk 8:21

Chapter Fifteen

Priorities

Strive first for the kingdom of God. Mt 6:33

As we saw in the case of attitudes to money and possessions in chapter 14, and his words about putting service to the kingdom ahead of family, Jesus requires more from those who join his band of disciples on the road than from the general population invited to join the kingdom, and even more from himself. Yet those more demanding standards tell us much about the values and priorities of the kingdom of God.

In Reading 15.1, Jesus is saying that God will provide, so his disciples are not to worry about where their next meal is coming from, or about their clothes, or about what tomorrow will bring. Instead, they must concentrate on the kingdom of God. Those of us who live in the world, and who cannot be disciples in the fuller sense, can at least take the implications of this teaching to heart and try to live accordingly.

In Reading 15.2, Paul lists some of the characteristics of the 'new self', which reflect those of the kingdom. Here, he concentrates on how the recipients of his letter should behave to each other, while in Reading 15.3, he condemns those who teach hidden mysteries and practise extra disciplines, arguing that the faithful he is addressing already have all that is required, namely 'The knowledge of God's mystery, that is, Christ himself.' *Col 2:2*

Reading 15.1
Why Do You Worry?
Therefore, I tell you, do not worry about your life, what you will eat, or about your body, what you will wear. Is not life more than food, and the body more than clothing? Consider the birds of the air, they neither sow nor reap, nor gather into barns, and yet our

heavenly Father feeds them. Are you not of more value than they? And can any of you by worrying add a single hour to your span of life? And why do you worry about clothing? Consider the lilies of the field, how they grow; they neither toil nor spin, yet I tell you, even Solomon in all his glory was not clothed like one of these. But if God so clothes the grass of the field, which is alive today and tomorrow is thrown into the oven, will he not much more clothe you – *you of little faith?* Therefore do not worry, saying, 'What will we eat?' or 'What will we drink?' or 'What will we wear?' ... Your heavenly Father knows that you need all these things. But strive first for the kingdom of God and his righteousness, and all these things will be given to you as well. So do not worry about tomorrow, for tomorrow will bring worries of its own. Today's trouble is enough for today. *Mt 6:25–34*

Reading 15.2
The new self
Clothe yourselves with the new self, created according to *the likeness of God* in true righteousness and holiness. So then, putting away falsehood, let all of us speak the truth to our neighbours, for we are members of one another. Be angry but do not sin; *do not let the sun go down on your anger* ... Thieves must give up stealing; rather let them labour and work honestly with their own hands, so as to have something to share with the needy. Let no evil talk come out of your mouths, but only what is useful for building up, as there is need, so that your words may give grace to those that hear ... Put away from you all bitterness and wrath and anger and wrangling and slander, together with all malice, and be kind to one another, tender-hearted, forgiving one another, as God in Christ has forgiven you. Therefore be imitators of God, and live in love. *Eph 4:24–5:2*

Reading 15.3
You have Christ himself
Do not let anyone disqualify you, insisting on self-abasement and worship of angels, dwelling on visions, puffed up without cause by a human way of thinking ... Why do you submit to regulations, 'Do not handle, do not taste, do not touch?' All these regulations refer to things that perish with use; they are simply human

commands and teaching. These have indeed an appearance of wisdom in promoting self-imposed piety, humility and severe treatment of the body, but they are of *no value* in checking self-indulgence. *Col 2:18–23*

Q *What sorts of religious/spiritual practices is Paul rejecting here?*

Chapter Sixteen

Love

'God is love.' (1 Jn 4:8)

Love lies behind many of the teachings we have looked at in this book. The Sermon on the Mount stresses love even of our enemies (Reading 10.1), social justice is about love of neighbour, including the stranger (Reading 11.2), and Jesus says that the loving behaviour of the female sinner is a sure sign she has been forgiven (Reading 12.1), while the loving father, like the loving God, forgives despite everything (Reading 12.3).

As one might expect, given the importance of the topic, the Readings in this section are all outstanding. In Reading 16.1, Jesus combines two sayings from the Old Testament, adding our duty to our fellow men and women to the requirement to love God. It is worth noting too that his teaching takes for granted that we love ourselves. Self-loathing plays no part in Christ's teaching.

Reading 16.2, the parable of the Good Samaritan, is Jesus' answer to the question 'Who is my neighbour?' It is probably the best-known of the parables and it illustrates why they are so effective and attractive. Unlike in an allegory, details are included for the sake of the story's effectiveness and characters do not represent anyone, they are themselves. It is obvious to all who hear (and read) this story what lesson is to be drawn from it: as Jesus puts it, they, and we, should go and act in the same loving way in our own particular circumstances. Note that he requires the person who asked the question to complete the answer himself. Typically, he makes the hero of the story a Samaritan, not a Jew, while the travellers who pass by without helping are members of the religious establishment with important jobs in the Temple at Jerusalem.

Paul's application of Jesus' teaching about love is justly famous (Reading 16.3). Writing to the church in the Greek city of Corinth where there has been factionalism and squabbling about the relative importance of various roles in the community, he makes it clear that love is more important than anything else. The list of the desirable characteristics associated with it no doubt tells us indirectly something about the problems within the Corinthian church and what was lacking in the behaviour of its members.

One of John's great themes is love and Reading 16.4 includes some of his teaching on that topic from his first letter. It may surprise you.

Reading 16.1
The greatest commandment

A lawyer asked him: 'Teacher, which commandment in the law is the greatest?' He said to him, 'You shall love the Lord God with *all your heart*, and with all your soul, and with all your mind.' This is the greatest and first commandment. And the second is like it: 'You shall love your neighbour as yourself.' On these two commandments hang all the law and the prophets. *Mt 22:36–40*

After hearing his answer, one of those present asks Jesus who his neighbour is and he answers indirectly but eloquently with this, his greatest parable, which has given our language the phrase 'to pass by on the other side' and the expression 'a good Samaritan'.

Reading 16.2
The Good Samaritan: a parable

Jesus replied, 'A man was going down from Jerusalem to Jericho, and fell into the hands of robbers, who stripped him, beat him, and went away, leaving him half-dead. Now by chance a priest was going down that road; and when he saw him, he passed by on the other side. So likewise a Levite, when he came to the place and saw him, passed by on the other side. The Samaritan while travelling came near him; and when he saw him, he was moved with pity. He went to him and bandaged his wounds, having poured out oil and wine on them. Then he put him on his own animal, brought him to an inn and took care of him. The next day he took out two denarii, gave them to the innkeeper and said 'Take care of him; and when I come back I will repay you whatever more you spend.' Which of these three, do you think, was a neighbour to the man who fell into the hands of robbers?' He said, 'The one who showed him mercy.' Jesus said to him, '*Go and do likewise.*' *Lk 10:30–37*

Reading 16.3
The greatest of these is love
If I speak in tongues of mortals and of angels, but do not have love, I am a noisy gong or a clanging cymbal. And if I have prophetic powers, and understand all mysteries and all knowledge, and if I have all faith so as to remove mountains, but do not have love, I am nothing. If I give away all my possessions, and if I hand over my body to be burned so that I may boast, but do not have love, I gain nothing.

Love is patient, love is kind; love is not envious or boastful or arrogant or rude. It does not insist on its own way; it is not irritable or resentful; it does not rejoice in wrongdoing, but rejoices in the truth. It bears all things, believes all things, endures all things ... Faith, hope and love abide, these three; and the greatest of these is love. *1 Cor 13:1–7, 13*

Reading 16.4
Love in the first letter of St John
Those who do not love a brother or sister whom they have seen, cannot love God whom they have not seen. The commandment we have from him is this:

> Those who love God must love their brothers and sisters also. (1 Jn 4:20–21)

> No one has ever seen God: if we love one another, God lives in us. (1 Jn 4:12)

> Those who abide in love abide in God, and God abides in them. (1 Jn 4:16)

> Let us love one another, because love is from God: everyone who loves is born of God and knows God. Whoever does not love does not know God, for *God is love*. (1 Jn 4:7–8)

These short extracts from the letters of St John have remarkable implications for anyone who tries to live by the gospel. Consider what they signify for you.

Chapter Seventeen

Prayer

In the morning, while it was still very dark, he got up and went out to a deserted place, and there he prayed. Mk 1:35

In this second part of the book, we have been considering what the New Testament documents have to say about Jesus' teaching and we have been doing so in the light of what we learned of his identity in the first part. The subject of prayer brings together both aspects. According to the prayer he teaches his disciples (Reading 17.1), the Father, his Father, is ours too. This is reflected in the teaching of John and Paul that we can all become sons and daughters of God through faith in Jesus (Readings 2.16 and 2.10 respectively). The prayer expresses hope for the coming of the kingdom of God, as outlined in chapter 9 and defined here in shorthand as God's will being done. The key element in putting the principles of the kingdom into practice is forgiveness (Chapter 12), by which we demonstrate our love for one another (Chapter 16).

In condemning wordiness, he gives this example of a short prayer, one which has been used by Christians ever since. The *Lord's Prayer* appears in slightly different forms in Luke and Matthew and it is the latter, longer form which has become the norm (there are some differences of translation between this version and the one generally used in prayer in English-speaking countries)

Reading 17.1 The Lord's Prayer
Pray then in this way: 'Our Father in heaven, hallowed be your name. Your kingdom come. Your will be done, on earth as it is in heaven. Give us this day our daily bread. And forgive us our debts, as we also have forgiven our debtors. And do not bring us to the time of trial, but rescue us from the evil one.' *Mt 6:9–13*

Jesus practises private prayer. To escape the pressure of the eager crowds who want to hear him speak or have him heal them, he 'would withdraw to deserted places and pray' (Lk 5:16; see also Mk 6:46). Sometimes he takes his closest followers with him, but then goes off alone, and a little further away (e.g. at the transfiguration, Lk 9:28–26; in the Garden of Gethsemane, 22:40–46).

He is also described as praying alone before the visions accompanying his baptism (the descent of the Holy Spirit in the form of a dove, Lk 3:21–22) and the transfiguration (Elijah and Moses talking to Jesus, Lk 9.28–29), as well as the moment when he asks the disciples who they think he is, which leads to Peter's declaration of faith (Lk 9:28–36), and as we have seen, in the garden shortly before his arrest. He does pray aloud to the Father, relatively rarely in the synoptics, frequently in the fourth gospel. His teaching on prayer (Reading 17.2) is that, like fasting, almsgiving and other good deeds, it should ideally not be done in public:

Reading 17.2 Pray in secret
Whenever you pray, do not be like the hypocrites; for they love to stand and pray in the synagogues and at the street corners, so that they may be seen by others ... When you pray, go into your room and shut the door and pray to your Father who is in secret; and your Father who sees in secret will reward you. *Mt 6:5–6*

This praise of private prayer (presumably it includes metaphorical 'secret rooms' as one goes about one's business during the day) is not to be taken as a criticism of liturgical prayer: Jesus attended his local synagogue every Saturday. However, if we are to take him as an example, private prayer in some form is necessary to the spiritual life. It is not enough to be righteous in conduct.

Reading 15.3 contains examples of simple, sincere prayer and its opposite in the mouths of the humble tax collector and the complacent Pharisee respectively. Jesus also tells two amusing parables worth looking at about perseverance in prayer, involving people making utter nuisances of themselves until they obtain satisfaction (Lk 11:5–8 and 18:1–7). His conclusion, as in his teaching on priorities in chapter 15, is not to worry and to have faith, as God is a loving Father: 'So I say to you, ask, and it will be given to you; search, and you will find; knock, and the door will be opened for you' Lk 11:9.

Gospel references
Lk 5:16; 9:28–36; 11:1–13; 18:1–7

Afterword

We can see different attempts at dealing with Jesus' identity within the New Testament. In a way, it is a work in progress. The background ranges from second coming to pre-existence. Given his identity as the messiah, the expectation in the synoptic gospels is that Jesus will return in glory 'at the end of the age' and so install a definitive, messianic version of the kingdom. In the meantime, the kingdom keeps breaking through, anticipating that final event. In another perspective, the resurrection is the crucial moment in revealing Jesus to be the only Son of the Father, vindicating his suffering at the crucifixion. We also see the parallel endorsements of Jesus as the beloved Son of God after his baptism and at the transfiguration, and the account of the revelation to Mary that the son she would bear would be the messiah and the Son of God. Adding to a complicated picture is the idea of pre-existence, that the Word was already 'with God' in the beginning. Finally, the relationship of the Father and the Son is not exclusive. The message of the scriptures is that all of us can become adopted sons or daughters of the same Father through faith in Jesus Christ, and so enter the kingdom of God which John calls eternal life.

A message about the Father
Whatever the evangelists mean by the phrase 'Son of God', a son presupposes a father and we need to remember that Jesus' message is not primarily about himself, it is about the Father, his father. The kingdom of God is the reign of the Father. In terms of the father/son metaphor at least, then, his identity depends directly on his Father's, it is defined by that relationship. In the more explicit style of John's gospel, Jesus repeatedly comes back to the relationship: to believe in him is to believe in the one who sent him; his teaching is not from him, but from the one who sent him; to have seen him is to have seen the Father; if you knew him,

you would know the Father as well; he and the Father are one; he is in the Father as the Father is in him. Yet he almost teasingly qualifies the impact of such statements when he adds that the Father is greater than he is.

The most decisive influence on the faith of his early followers, including the authors of the scriptures themselves, were the accounts of the resurrection experiences of the disciples, coupled with their own experience of the ongoing sacramental presence of the risen Jesus in the Eucharist. To the New Testament authors we have been reading, Jesus could not be closer to the Father, he is like an only son or a word uttered by the mouth of God, to use two analogies from one of them; like a perfect copy or image of the unseen God, to use another author's metaphor. Jesus is called God only once in the gospels, in response to an appearance of the risen Christ (see Chapter 6). The New Testament definitions can be summarised by saying that Jesus is completely God-orientated. As far as the Christian church was concerned, eventually adopting as a doctrine that Jesus was both fully human and the incarnate Word, the Son of God, involved a modification of the idea of God so that it could accommodate the Son alongside the Father and the Holy Spirit in a Trinity.

Authority and integrity

The Readings in this book make it clear that Jesus Christ inspired people to follow him principally by the unique authority and integrity of his person and his teaching. Everything else flows from these characteristics, which are anyway interconnected. The story itself comes full circle from the gathering together of a small band of men and women in Galilee to the similarly small group of disciples who experience the resurrection. On the way, Jesus attracts ever larger and more demanding crowds, until the religious leadership takes fright, and involves the Romans. When the inevitable crisis comes, the crowds desert him, as do his disciples. Throughout, the background to the story is dominated by the public impact of his ministry. The same applies after his death: his works and words were remembered and recorded alongside the narrative of his suffering, death and resurrection, by the small community he left behind and those of the next generation who responded to their preaching as Christianity grew and spread with amazing rapidity. He still inspires men and women who encounter him in the scriptures and in the Eucharist.

That is about as far as the scriptures can take us. The rest is down to opinions – or faith. I hope this book has helped you to look anew at Jesus Christ. Whatever conclusion you come to about him, it must account for 'the light of the knowledge of the glory of God' in his face.

A note on miracles

The four gospels are free of the fantastic and at times grotesque magic often found in popular legends, even pious ones. Indeed, a reader expecting frequent miracles in the gospels will be disappointed. Jesus' many acts of healing depend on the faith of the sick person and some are obviously also symbolic (see Readings 4.1 and 4.2 and the accompanying notes). You can read the gospels for yourself and make up your own mind about them, as well as the exorcisms and the story of the marriage feast at Cana (Jn 2:1-12). However, there are three sets of events in the gospels which do call for some further comment.

Raising the dead

A widow's son (Lk 7:11ff), Jairus' daughter (Lk 8:40ff) and Lazarus (Jn 11:1ff) are all restored to life by Jesus. Lazarus and his sisters Martha and Mary are friends of Jesus and the miracle comes shortly before Jesus' arrest and execution and so can be regarded as in some sense looking ahead to his own resurrection, and revealing his power over death. However, the other two cases come early in his ministry and Jesus does not know the families. In the first he feels sorry for the dead man's mother while in the second, the girl's father begs him for help while she is still alive.

Feeding the 5000 (and then the 4000): Mk 6:30–44 and 8:1–10; Mt 14:13–21 and 15:32–39

Scholars conclude that either these are two versions of the same story or that there is a symbolic difference between them, for example one event for Jews and one for gentiles. That they have been preserved possibly in different traditions and then both included in the gospels of Mark and Matthew indicates their significance for the evangelists (although Luke and John each include only one account). Whatever originally lies behind them, they would come to be seen as referring to the Eucharist.

Walking on the water (e.g. Mt 14:22–33)

What strikes you immediately about the story is the clear echo of a notable feature of some of Jesus' post-resurrection appearances (see Readings 6.1 and 6.2 and accompanying notes): namely, that the disciples present simply do not recognise Jesus. In this case, they think they are seeing a ghost until he speaks, and Peter loses confidence when trying to follow Jesus and has to be helped. This reinforces the story's point, which is about faith and the lack of it.

Books of the Bible
used in the Readings
or referred to in the notes

OLD TESTAMENT

Genesis (Gen)
The first book of the Jewish Bible, it begins with an account of the creation (Reading 2.1) and the disobedience of the first human couple. It also introduces the story of the common ancestor of the Jewish people, Abraham. Reading 1:1–3.

Deuteronomy (Deut)
The fifth and final book of the Pentateuch which, together with commentaries on it, constitutes the Jewish law (Reading 2.2). The book ends with the death of Moses, having brought his people out of slavery in Egypt, through the desert to the very borders of the Promised Land. The violent partisanship attributed to the God of the Hebrews as his people conquer and take over the lands of those already living in the territory he has set aside for them can be profoundly shocking. Reading 30:11–14.

Psalms (Ps)
The hymnbook of ancient Judaism, adopted by Christianity. Overall, the most accessible book in the OT, although it too occasionally includes sentiments and topics such as glorying in revenge which seem unworthy of a God who demands ethical behaviour from his followers. Readings from Psalms 19, 27, 40, 139, 146.

Isaiah (Isa)
The book of Isaiah is the work of successive authors with a gap of 150 years or so preceding and following the exile of the Jewish people in Babylon (First Isaiah, Chapters 1 to 40; Second and Third Isaiah, Chapters 40–55, and 56–66). In the first case, the prophet is warning his people, including its rulers, of disasters to come unless they return to the ways of the Law. Afterwards, he offers them consolation by looking forward to the rebuilding of Jerusalem in better times, closing with a vision of all the nations united in the service of the one God. It is constantly referred to both explicitly and implicitly in the New Testament, including by Jesus (e.g. Reading 3.1), and in the figure of the Suffering Servant (see Reading 5.1 and notes) decisively influenced how the suffering and execution of Jesus were interpreted. Readings 53:4–6; 55:8–9; 59:9–11; 60:1.

Jeremiah (Jer)
With Isaiah, the greatest prophet: both are particularly associated with the development of what is called ethical monotheism, the idea that the God of the Jews is the only one there is and that what pleases him above all is ethical behaviour. Jeremiah was active in the 600s BC, the final years before the conquest of the surviving Jewish kingdom and the exile of many of its people. He warned his fellow Jews that they were bringing a catastrophe down on themselves by their turning away from God, and used powerful and at times shocking imagery of sexual faithlessness to describe their behaviour. He also held out the hopeful prospect of a new covenant with God which would be written on the hearts of men and women. Reading: Jer 1:4–9.

Wisdom/Ecclesiasticus/Proverbs (Wis, Prov)
Under the influence of Greek thought in Alexandria, the Judaism of the late OT period developed its own form of wisdom literature in which *Sophia* or Wisdom is personified in female form and seen as the handmaiden of God or equated with the Law. In turn, Wisdom influenced the idea of the Word in John and Paul's metaphors for the identity of Jesus (see notes in Chapter 2a).

The identities of the evangelists are by no means certain. Traditionally, Mark was thought to be one of the companions of Paul on his missionary journeys. Matthew was assumed to be the tax collector called Levi in Luke's gospel but Matthew elsewhere. The author known as Luke certainly wrote both the gospel of that name and the Acts of the Apostles, but, apart from a tradition that he was a doctor, nothing is known of him. It seems unlikely that the evangelist John is the same person as the apostle of that name: his gospel's use of Greek ideas also makes it unlikely that the writer was the Galilean fisherman called by Jesus. As you will see below, some of the letters attributed to St Paul are generally considered to be rather the work of followers writing with his authority or in his tradition, while the letter to the Hebrews is universally accepted as being by an unknown author.

THE SYNOPTIC GOSPELS

Gospel according to Mark (Mk)
Generally held to be the first of the gospels to be written, possibly in Rome in the AD 60s, it was therefore available to the other synoptic evangelists, who both used it as a source alongside others. Mark's is also the shortest gospel and does not include any material about the birth or infancy of Jesus or any post-resurrection appearances; in fact, it ends abruptly when the women discover that the tomb is empty. It also begins quite dramatically with the preaching of John the Baptist and the baptism of Jesus (Introductory Reading 1). Mark particularly stresses Jesus' activity as a healer (Readings 4.1 and 4.2 and notes). Another feature of this gospel is 'the messianic secret': Jesus is most anxious not to reveal he is the Messiah until the time is ripe, perhaps because of the differing expectations of the nature of the messiah in the Jewish community, as the gospel was written for gentile Christians. According to tradition, 'Mark' had privileged access to material from Peter. Readings: Mk 1:11; 4:24–34; 10:46–52.

Gospel according to Matthew (Mt)
Written in or near Judea for Jewish Christians. It was probably designed for instruction or preaching and as a guide to church

government (see Chapter 18 in particular). The author handles the items in his sources (including Mark and a collection of the sayings of Jesus) with skill: see for example the artificial compilation from his sources known as the Sermon on the Mount (Chapter 5 of his gospel, Reading 9.1 and notes). Readings: 5:17, 21–28; 6:6, 9–13, 19–21, 24, 25–34; 7:24–29; 11:28–30, 25; 16:24; 17:1–8; 21:9–13, 33–40; 22:36–40; 25:1–13, 31–40; 26:36–46; 28:19–20.

Gospel according to Luke (Lk)
The first of a two-part work including the Acts of the Apostles. It was probably written in Antioch (in modern Turkey, on the Syrian border) by a Gentile convert to Christianity, drawing on Mark's gospel and a collection of sayings, and who also had a link with the tradition which was responsible for the gospel of John. The author is the best writer of the four evangelists and is particularly skilful at major set-piece narratives such as Readings 3.1, 12.1 and 16.3 or the infancy stories in the first two chapters (introductory Reading 2). He is also anxious to do justice to the place of women among Jesus' followers (e.g. Reading 6.1 and notes). Readings: Lk 1:30–35; 4:16–21; 5:17, 21–28, 27–32; 6:27–30, 32–35, 43–45; 7:36–50; 10:30–37; 12:16–21; 13:10–17; 14:16–20; 11:11–32; 18:9–14, 15–17, 20–25; 19:1–10; 24:30–35.

THE FOURTH GOSPEL

Gospel according to John (Jn)
The last of the gospels to be written, probably in Asia Minor (the Western part of modern Turkey) in the AD 90s. It is closer in places to Luke than to the other two synoptics but probably represents a largely independent tradition. In his gospel, John insistently stresses Jesus' relationship with the Father and is anxious above all to communicate the spiritual significance of the events of Jesus' life and ministry, using first person statements by Jesus to do so ('I am the bread of life' and similar: see Introduction to Part One). The gospel opens with a prologue (Reading 2.16) in which Jesus is presented as the Word of God become man. This, the mystery of the incarnation, is particularly stressed in John's gospel, along with the Eucharist, the role of the Holy Spirit once Jesus

returns to the Father, and love as a distinguishing mark of Jesus' followers (Reading 16.4). The evangelist uses the term 'eternal life' where the authors of the synoptic gospels tend to speak of 'the Kingdom of God', he does not include the institution of the eucharist in his account of the Last Supper and places the cleansing of the Temple at the start, rather than the end, of Jesus' ministry. Readings: Jn 1:1–18; 5:24; 8:3–11; 11:45–47; 12:44–46; 14:27; 20:14–18.

LETTERS OF PAUL

Paul was originally a fierce enemy of Christianity who became one of its leaders after a vision of Jesus. In particular, he favoured taking the gospel to the gentiles. He, and followers writing in his name or on his behalf, wrote letters to churches all over the eastern Mediterranean, many of which he had set up himself. In the letters, he is often answering questions or commenting on a dispute rather than writing in a considered way about a subject in all its aspects. He was probably executed in Rome in about AD 65. There are Readings from, or references in the notes to, the letters to the:

Galatians (c.54 AD) (Gal)
Paul has to combat those in the local church in Galatia, in modern Turkey, who insist that converts to Christianity must be circumcised, including non-Jews. Reading: *Gal* 3:26–29.

Corinthians (First letter) (c.AD 54) (1 Cor)
Paul first has to deal with squabbling and factionalism in the local church in the great Greek city of Corinth. He then answers a list of questions on sexual morality, marriage, contact with pagans, behaviour in church and other matters submitted by members of the congregation, before ending with some teaching on the resurrection. This early letter is written in the certainty that Christ will return soon and that the world will then end, a perspective one must bear in mind when reading it. Contains famous passages about love (Reading 16.3) and the Eucharist (Reading 7.1). Readings: 1 Cor 11:23–28; 13:1–7, 13.

Romans (c.AD 57) (Rom)
The letter contains a long and fascinating argument about his pride in being a Jew and a Pharisee and, despite that, believing that gentiles should be accepted throughout the church without the need for circumcision or any of the other requirements of the Law. He argues that what matters above all is faith in Jesus Christ (notes on Reading 5.1). Paul did not set up the church in the capital of the Empire and at the time of writing had not yet visited it.

Colossians (AD 70–80) (Col), probably the work of a follower of Paul, begins with and develops what was already an established hymn about Jesus as the image of God. Reading: Col 2:18–22.

Ephesians (AD 80–100) (Eph), probably the work of a follower of Paul, deals with the ideas of the church (already seen as an institution, rather than simply a scattering of individual churches) as the body of Christ and as the bride of Christ. Reading: Eph 4:22–5:2.

First Letter to Timothy (AD 80s or 90s) (1 Tim), probably the work of a follower of Paul. Timothy was a leading colleague of Paul, given here as the recipient of this letter. The author is probably using Paul's name to add weight to its argument against heretical tendencies in the church, the so-called 'false teachers'.

OTHER LETTERS

Letter to the Hebrews (AD 70-90) (Heb)
The unknown author writes about the old covenant having been replaced by the new, with Jesus, the Son of God, as its high priest (notes on Reading 5.1). Readings: Heb 1:1–3; 4:12–13.

First Letter of John (c.AD 90) (1 Jn)
Echoes the distinctive tone of John's gospel, with its stress on love (see Reading 16.4). Readings: 1 Jn 4:10, 12, 20–21, 7–8.

Letter of James (c.AD 100) (Jas)
The author is a Jewish Christian particularly concerned that faith should be translated into action (works). He writes in the name

of James, the Brother of the Lord, leader of the Jerusalem church, executed in AD 62. Reading: Jas 2:14–17.

Second Letter of Peter (c.AD 100 or later) (2 Pet)
The author claims to be the apostle but for various reasons we can be reasonably sure that he is not. The letter aims to reassure the faithful about the apparent delay in the Second Coming of Christ.

IN A CATEGORY OF ITS OWN

Acts of the Apostles (AD 80-90) (Acts)
Luke's account of the early years in the life of the church, starting from the ascension of Jesus, and with a particular focus on the missionary activity of Paul.

Revelation (c.AD 95) (Rev)
An example of apocalyptic, features of which are prophecy and complex symbolism. Following a bloody period of persecution, it understandably attacks the Roman Empire (disguised as Babylon) and celebrates the victory of the sacrificial Lamb, Jesus. Reading: Rev 3:20.

Where to next?
If you want to read some more of the scriptures, you can explore the books featuring in these Readings or follow up the references in the notes. If you want to read a whole gospel, I would recommend Luke for his skill as a scene-setter and storyteller. If you want examples you need only turn to Readings such as 3.1, 11.1 and the way he presents the parables of the Good Samaritan and the Prodigal Son. After reading Luke, you could then go on to the other document he contributed to the New Testament, the *Acts of the Apostles,* a lively account, including some sermons, of St Paul's tireless and wide-ranging missionary work building up the church among the gentiles. The most immediately accessible material in the OT is the great poetic treasure house of the *Psalms.*

To find out more about the background to the gospels or the New Testament in general, invest in a *biblical commentary*. If your interest lies more in the direction of how the church developed in the succeeding centuries, you will find two excellent books give you the framework you need: *Christianity: The first two thousand years* by David L. Edwards (London, Cassell: 1997) and *Christian Theology: An Introduction* by Alister E. McGrath (Oxford, Blackwell: 1994 and subsequent editions). Mainstream Christian teaching is accessibly laid out in *The Catechism of the Catholic Church* (London, Geoffrey Chapman: 1994).

By far the best film based on the gospel story is Pasolini's *The Gospel according to St Matthew*, despite (or because of) the fact that he was not a Christian.

Bibliography

All books are suitable for beginners and general readers

Avis, P., *God and the Creative Imagination: Metaphor, Symbol and Myth in Religion and Theology* (Abingdon, 1999).

Barton, J., ed., *The Oxford Bible Commentary* (Oxford, 2001).

Brown, R. et al., *The New Jerome Bible Commentary* (London, 1995).

Burridge, R., *Four Gospels, One Jesus? A Symbolic Reading* (London, 2005).

Edwards, D.L., *Christianity: The First Two Thousand Years* (London, 1997).

Foster, D., *Reading with God: Lectio Divina* (London, 2005).

Gunton, C., *The Actuality of Atonement: A Study of Metaphor, Rationality and the Christian Tradition* (London, 1988).

Hogan, M.P., *Seeking Jesus of Nazareth: An Introduction to the Christology of the Four Gospels* (Dublin, 2001).

McGrath, A., *Christian Theology: An Introduction* (Second Edition, Malden Mass and Oxford, 1997).

Stanton, C.M., *The Gospels and Jesus* (Second Edition, Oxford, 2002).

Vermes, G., *Jesus the Jew* (London, 1983).

Lectio Divina: *Group Meditation*

If you found focused reading useful, then you will probably be interested in this reading-based method of meditation, currently undergoing a worldwide revival.

While *Lectio Divina* is well suited to individual meditation, membership of a group gives it an extra dynamic. The combined silence of half a dozen people is almost tangible and the different insights and conclusions of the other participants always stimulating. First you need a group leader or coordinator, whether on a regular basis and/or rotating among the various group members. He or she makes sure copies of the readings are available, leads a group into its preliminary relaxation exercise, then slowly reads out the meditation text without distributing a copy (so that everybody concentrates on what they're hearing), then after a short pause either reads it through again or asks a member of the group to do so. Only then is the text given out. During meditation, group members can re-read sections or refresh their memories by glancing at the text.

The coordinator brings the silent meditation session to an end at the agreed time and then encourages anyone with an insight or comment they wish to share to do so, while making sure that those who do not wish, or feel unable to contribute publicly, feel under no pressure to do so. The simplest way to begin this section of the session is to ask participants which words or phrases in the text caught their attention and then to go back and ask some at least if they could outline to the group where that phrase or word took them during the meditation. This is always enlightening. The group leader keeps an eye on the time and closes the whole session with a summing-up in the form of a prayer drawing on the contributions of everyone present if possible.

Icons

An icon can fulfil the same function as a candle, enabling you to focus and so resist more effectively the distractions thrown up by a hyperactive mind.

The instantly recognisable iconic image of the Madonna and Child is perhaps the most popular religious image of our civilisation. It derives its power from its representation of the closest of human relationships in the context of the incarnation: this helpless child is the only Son of God.

To most people an icon is an image on a computer representing a programme or application. Some will also know that icons are also works of art representing Jesus Christ and episodes from his life, also Mary, especially holding the Christ child in her arms, and the saints. They are associated principally with Orthodox Christianity, Greek and Russian, and are highly stylised. Art, like music, can move us at a deeper level than words. A piece written hundreds of years ago by a German church musician can move 21st-century agnostics to tears. To express ourselves more fully and to communicate at a deeper level we need symbols, rituals and images.

Icons are part of a living tradition: each painter expresses himself or herself within the constraints of the tradition when it comes to the choice of colours and the posture of the figures. Traditions in this context are the very opposite of the dead hand of the past on the artist's shoulder – they give the artist a framework in which he or she can communicate across the ages, enabling him or her to concentrate on expressing as effectively and as beautifully as possible the familiar figure, scene or spiritual truth.

Iconoclasm (literally the breaking of images, as happened in the Reformation in England) derives in the end from an exaggerated fear of representing spiritual entities in images. Icons and similar religious objects are not idols, they are not worshipped.

You probably carry around with you in your purse or wallet or have on your desk or bedside table a photo of someone dear to you. You may even take it out and look at it or talk to it. You may kiss it. The person the photo represents may be living or dead, they may be hundreds of miles away or tucked up in bed at home, but in a sense they are with you.

The same goes for other symbols and images. The soldier saluting the flag is honouring his country, not the piece of cloth symbolising it. And it is what they symbolise that matters. An icon, crucifix or statue is honoured and revered because of what it represents. We know in our hearts that beauty expresses a truth about the divine. An icon is perfect for calm contemplation without words.

Candles and Meditation

Candles are probably the single most effective aid to reflection, meditation and prayer. In particular, they help with focusing the attention and emptying the mind or avoiding distractions. The flame holds your attention and even remains visible when you close your eyes. It also symbolises the presence of Jesus Christ.

The best-known example of that symbolic use is during the Easter vigil service. The Paschal (Easter) candle is lit outside the darkened church and is then taken inside in a joyful procession which stops three times to allow the cantor to proclaim 'The light of Christ!' and members of the congregation to light their small, hand-held candles, directly or indirectly, from the Paschal candle. Eventually the church is filled with Easter light and the Paschal candle is installed on the altar where it will remain until the feast of the ascension six weeks later, a symbol of the risen Lord's presence among his disciples in the time after his resurrection

Glossary and list of names

Abba	'Father' in Aramaic, Jesus' mother tongue.
Allegory	Story in which each character and situation stands for another.
Anna	Priest who recognises the infant Jesus as the Messiah.
Annunciation	When the angel tells Mary she will be the mother of the Messiah. Celebrated on 25 March, nine months before Christmas Day.
Apostle	Greek: 'messenger'. Used of the inner group of 12 disciples, also of Paul, who was a later convert.
Annas	High priest.
Ascension	Jesus' return to the Father after his post-resurrection appearances.
Atonement	Making good the damage done by sin.
Baptism	John the Baptist: a ceremony symbolising repentance; in Christianity, the sacrament marking reception into the church.
Bethany	Town near Jerusalem.
Bible	The Christian Bible comprises two parts: the Old Testament and the New.
Caiaphas	High priest.
Cephas	Aramaic for 'rock', alternative name for Peter, itself from the Greek for 'rock'.
Centurion	Officer commanding 100 men.
Christ of faith	Jesus as portrayed in the scriptures: see 'Jesus of history'.
Covenant	The special relationship between God and the Jewish people.

Crib	A scene representing the new-born Jesus, Mary and Joseph with shepherds and the three Magi or kings who have come to worship him in the stable, all watched over by an ox and an ass.
Crucifixion	Roman method of execution in which the victim was left to die hanging on a cross.
Disciple	A follower of a spiritual leader or teacher.
Easter Sunday	The feast day on which the resurrection is celebrated.
Emmanuel	Hebrew name: 'God is with us'.
Emmaus	Village near Jerusalem.
Eternal life	The equivalent of the kingdom of God in St John's gospel.
Elijah	Prophet who appears with Moses in the transfiguration. He was expected to come again as a forerunner of the Messiah.
Eucharist	Another term for Holy Communion.
Exile	The period when a remnant of the Jewish people was forcibly sent to live in Babylon after a military defeat interpreted by the prophets Isaiah and Jeremiah as the consequence of turning away from the Law.
Evangelist	Author of a gospel.
Father	Jesus' name for God.
Fourth	The gospel of John, distinguishing it from the Gospel synoptics.
Galilee	Region to the North of Samaria and Judaea with a mixed population of Jews and Gentiles. Jesus grew up and launched his ministry there.
Gentile	A non-Jew.
Gethsemane	Garden in which Jesus spent the time between the Last Supper and his arrest in prayer.
Good Friday	The day marking Jesus' death.
High Priest	Religious leader of the Jewish people.

Holy	Christian sacrament commemorating Communion the Last Supper.
Holy One of God	The Messiah.
Holy Spirit	The enlivening presence of God after Jesus returns to the Father, particularly among the disciples.
Incarnation	Literally 'en-flesh-ment': a term taken from St John's gospel where he says the 'Word (Jesus) became flesh', that is became a human being.
Infancy gospel or narrative:	The first two chapters of Luke and Matthew, focusing on the circumstances of Jesus' conception and birth.
Isaiah	Greatest of the prophets, much quoted in the NT.
Jairus	Official of a synagogue, Jesus restores his daughter to life.
James	One of the twelve apostles, brother of John.
Jeremiah	Second most famous of the OT prophets.
Jerusalem	City. Seat of the Temple, the spiritual centre of Judaism.
Jesus of history	The 'real' Jesus Christ behind the gospel accounts of healings and miracles, assuming he can be found.
John the Apostle	One of the twelve apostles, brother of James.
John the Baptist	Religious figure who preached baptism for the forgiveness of sins; Jesus is baptised by him at the start of his ministry.
John the Evangelist	Author of the fourth gospel.
Judaea	The heartland of Judaism, centred on Jerusalem.
Justified	Made righteous.
Kingdom of God	God's rule: Jesus' preaching called for repentance as a precondition for entering the Kingdom.
Kingdom of Heaven	Alternative name for the Kingdom of God, avoiding direct use of the divine name out of respect.
Lamb of God	Symbolism: Jesus seen as a sacrificial Passover lamb.

Last Judgement	When all of humanity is gathered before the throne of God at the end of time.
Last Supper	Jesus' last meal with his followers on the evening of his arrest, known as Maunday or Holy Thursday, the day before his trial and execution, commemorated on Good Friday.
The Law	The first five books of the Jewish Bible.
Lazarus	Brother of Martha and Mary, restored to life by Jesus.
Leper	Person suffering from leprosy or a similar skin disease. Regarded with horror in biblical times.
Letters/Epistles	NT documents, letters sent by Paul, John and others to churches and individuals.
Levi/Matthew	Tax collector called by Jesus to follow him.
Levite	Official carrying out duties in the Temple.
Martha	Sister of Lazarus and Mary.
Mary	Mother of Jesus.
Mary	Sister of Martha and Lazarus, anoints Jesus' feet.
Mary Magdalene	Leading female disciple, witness to the Resurrection.
Matthew, Mark, Luke	Authors of the first three ('synoptic') gospels.
Messiah	Hoped-for deliverer of the Jewish people.
Messianic	To do with the messiah.
Metanoia	Greek 'new mind', conversion, translated as 'repentance', the precondition for entering the Kingdom of God.
Monotheism	Belief that there is only one God.
Moses	Patriarch of the Jewish people who led them out of slavery in Egypt.
The Nativity	Birth of Jesus Christ.
Nazareth	Town in Galilee where Jesus was brought up.
New Testament	Second part of the Bible; the specifically Christian scriptures. Abbreviated NT.

The One Who Is to Come	The Messiah.
Old Testament	First part of the Bible, the Jewish Scriptures (OT).
Parable	A story with a moral but freer than an allegory.
Paul	Originally a bitter enemy of Christianity, after his conversion he argued for and led the mission to the gentiles. He wrote letters of guidance and encouragement to various local churches as Christianity spread rapidly.
Pentecost	From the Greek for 'fifty'. The feast is fifty days after Easter. It celebrates the descent of the Holy Spirit on the followers of Jesus.
Peter	A fisherman chosen by Jesus to become leader of the disciples. Originally called Simon.
Pharisees	Members of the dominant faction in Judaism in NT times. Harshly criticised by Jesus.
Pontius Pilate	Roman prefect (governor) of Judaea.
Prophets	Jewish spiritual leaders who spoke on behalf of God.
Psalms	Book of Jewish religious poetry in the Bible.
Rabbi/Rabbouni	Hebrew/Aramaic: 'teacher'.
Redemption	Purchase of a slave's freedom: a metaphor for salvation.
Resurrection	Jesus' triumph over death, marked by the empty tomb and appearances to followers.
Sabbath	Seventh day of the week, Saturday. A day of rest for Jews.
Sacrament	Outward sign of an inner spiritual event e.g. Holy Communion (receiving bread and wine) or Baptism (symbolic bathing in water). The Catholic and Orthodox traditions recognise seven sacraments, the Protestant tradition only these two.
Samaritan	Inhabitant of Samaria in the north of the Holy Land. The Samaritans were regarded as heretics by Jews.

Scripture(s)	Sacred book(s) of a religion.
Scribes	Scholars/lawyers who interpreted the Law.
Second Coming	The return of Jesus at the end of time to reign as Messiah and judge all humanity.
Servant of the Lord	See Suffering Servant.
Scapegoat	The symbolic bearer of the sins of the people, released into the desert every year on the Day of Atonement.
Simeon	Prophet who had been told that he would not die until he had seen the Messiah (Lk, Chapter 2).
Son of David	The Messiah was expected to be descended from King David, the greatest king Israel had known.
Son of Man	Term used by Jesus to refer to himself.
Suffering servant	A symbolic figure in the prophecies of Isaiah, identified with Jesus Christ by Christians.
Synagogue	Jewish meeting house for prayer.
Synoptic	Greek 'seen together', name given to the first three gospels because they can be read together in three columns as they have so many verses in common or with only minor differences.
Temple	Until AD 70 the centre of the Jewish religion.
The Ten Commandments	Religious and moral code given to Moses on Mount Sinai.
Trinity	The Christian doctrine that in the one God there are three 'persons', Father, Son and Holy Spirit.
Wisdom literature	OT theme of Wisdom personified as a female figure, found in the Books of Job, Proverbs, Ecclesiasticus/Sirach, Wisdom.
Word	In the NT, the Word of God become flesh in Jesus Christ.
Zacchaeus	Rich senior tax collector who climbs a tree to see Jesus and is called down by him. He later makes good all he has stolen and gives generously to the poor.
Zechariah	Father of John the Baptist, priest in the Temple.